Mothering Special Needs

of related interest

Building a Joyful Life with your Child who has Special Needs
Nancy J. Whiteman and Linda Roan-Yager
ISBN 978 1 84310 841 2

Parenting Across the Autism Spectrum
Unexpected Lessons We Have Learned
Maureen F. Morrell and Ann Palmer
ISBN 978 1 84310 807 8

The Complete Guide to Asperger's Syndrome
Tony Attwood
ISBN 978 1 84310 495 7

Encouraging Appropriate Behavior for Children on the Autism Spectrum
Frequently Asked Questions
Shira Richman
ISBN 978 1 84310 825 2

Different Dads
Fathers' Stories of Parenting Disabled Children
Edited by Jill Harrison, Matthew Henderson and Rob Leonard
Foreword by Rt. Hon. David Cameron MP
ISBN 978 1 84310 454 4

Prevention and Coping in Child and Family Care
Mothers in adversity coping with child care
Michael Sheppard
With Mirka Gröhn
ISBN 978 1 84310 193 2

The ADHD Handbook
A Guide for Parents and Professionals
Alison Munden and Jon Arcelus
ISBN 978 1 85302 756 7

Mothering Special Needs

A Different Maternal Journey

Anna Karin Kingston

Foreword by Christopher Gillberg

Jessica Kingsley Publishers
London and Philadelphia

First published in 2007
by Jessica Kingsley Publishers
116 Pentonville Road
London N1 9JB, UK
and
400 Market Street, Suite 400
Philadelphia, PA 19106, USA

www.jkp.com

Printed digitally since 2009

Library of Congress Cataloging in Publication Data

Kingston, Anna Karin, 1961-

Mothering special needs : a different maternal journey / Anna Karin Kingston ; foreword by Christopher Gillberg.

p. cm.

Includes bibliographical references and index.

ISBN 978-1-84985-430-6 (alk. paper)

1. Parents of children with disabilities--Ireland. 2. Parents of developmentally disabled children-- Ireland. 3. Parents of autistic children--Ireland. 4. Mothers--Ireland. 5. Motherhood--Ireland. I. Title.

HQ759.913.K55 2007

306.874'3087409417--dc22

2007007807

British Library Cataloguing in Publication Data

A CIP catalogue record for this book is available from the British Library

ISBN 978 1 84985 430 6

To Alexander and Louisa

Acknowledgements

This book owes its existence to the 18 mothers participating in this project. I would like to thank each and every one of them for giving of their precious time and sharing their stories with me. I also want to thank the mothers in my support group for inspiring me to do this research by 'telling it as it is'. Thanks particularly to our counsellor Margaret Reid who empowered me when I needed it most. The substantial financial support from the Irish Research Council for Humanities and Social Sciences (IRCHSS) enabled me to pursue this research and I am honoured to have received this scholarship. I also acknowledge the smaller grant awarded to me by the National Disability Authority. Finally, my thanks go to all people involved in sharing the mothering of my two children with me, particularly Audrey O'Neill and Margaret O'Neill, but most of all Brian. Thanks for your eternal optimism and for stepping into 'motherhood' when you really had to!

Contents

Foreword

All parents make different life journeys and mothers of children with lifelong disabilities are no exception. But the difference is different in that such mothers, and such mothers only, are *expected* – by legislators, doctors, psychologists, social workers, teachers and clergy, indeed by everyone – to be the ultimate good mother, caring both *for* and *about* the child with the disability for the rest of their lives without ever intimating (much less pronouncing) the obvious: 'But hey, what about me?'

Anna Karin Kingston has decided to speak up and let the voices of mothers be heard instead of those of the specialists who might label them angry, depressed, over-protective (!) or even bad. It is a chilling book, reporting on several years of in-depth research with eighteen Irish mothers of children with Down syndrome, autism and ADHD. It is angry, sad, shocking, clear-headed and – ultimately – optimistic. It relates verbatim the scandal of how even the so-called modern society turns its back on mothers of disabled children and 'pretends that it just doesn't see'. It should be required reading for all involved in supporting families who struggle with lifelong disability.

Christopher Gillberg, MD, PhD
Professor of Child and Adolescent Psychiatry

Prologue

I knew I took a chance bringing him to the shopping centre. Two days previously he had absconded from the park, running in his bare feet to the other side of the city, eventually found and picked up by the police. My seven-year-old son, blond and blue-eyed, whose special needs had dramatically changed my life.

We arrived at the shopping centre together with my mother and my daughter, and trouble started almost immediately. At the trolleys he threw off his shoes and flung the coin into the shrubs. He scaled the long line of trolleys and was on his way to disappear out of my sight again. I asked my mother to go into the supermarket and start the shopping, while I chased after this wild child out of control. At the age of seven he was already very strong and agile and I knew that the shopping was over as far as he was concerned. The only thing I could do was to try to keep him safe and prevent him from running away from me again. I grabbed him by the arms and dragged him to the car. He fought like an animal, bit my hands, kicked and scrawled. I knew that if I put him inside the car he would break everything he could get hold of – levers for indicators and lights, the gear stick, the rear view mirror. So I opened the boot of the car and managed to get him in there and closed it. Panting and sweating, wiping the blood off my hands, I caught my breath and looked around.

A woman with a child in a buggy was looking at me, terrified and crying: 'Please, please, he's only a child. You can't do that to him, I know that you're upset, but you can't do that to a child!' she said. 'I have to ring the guards!' and she held her mobile phone up to her ear. I was still out of breath but this unexpected interference evoked even more anger and frustration and I snarled at her: 'If there was proper support in this country for children like him I wouldn't be in this situation!' At the same time I opened the boot to show her that I was not going to keep him locked in there for long. But as this child of mine was autistic, the confinement of the boot was one of his favourite places. This is where he hid himself many times. The snug, silent darkness of the boot was often his escape from a noisy and demanding world. This time was no exception, apart from the fact that I was going to be punished by him.

And as always, he was a step ahead of me and found something that could be damaged inside in the boot. After several attempts to get him to come out of the boot: 'Listen, there's a Mummy here and she is crying because you are in the boot, would you please come out or else she'll ring the guards!' he eventually stuck his head out, triumphantly holding the leads to the loudspeakers that he had just ripped off.

I got him to leave the boot and move into the car. He was calm now and agreed to rest in the back seat while I went into the supermarket to quickly finish the shopping. I ran in and asked my mother to go out and watch the car and make sure that he remained inside. While I ran around the supermarket with my daughter in the trolley, the upset woman contacted the security guards of the shopping centre. My mother told me how they came out to the car park, looked inside the car and saw a peaceful little boy lying in the back seat. They asked my mother if she knew the boy and she nodded, 'He's my grandchild'. We returned home to safety and I decided that I could no longer take the risk of bringing him shopping. As many times before, I had to rearrange my lifestyle to conform to the world of mothers living with special needs children.

I did not reflect more over the crying woman with the buggy until one week later when a policeman rang. He said that they had been given the registration number of our car by a woman who had reported a case of child abuse. Was it our car and had I put a child in the boot? I spent the following week preparing for my 'defence' by writing a letter explaining the circumstances. Our child was in the care of a service provider with a social worker already involved in our case. I also wanted the police to inform the woman that I fully understood her worry and that I admired her for having had the courage to interfere. Too many children suffer abuse at the hands of adults and the only way to prevent this from happening is for people to react exactly the way this particular woman reacted when she saw me putting my son in the boot.

My defence, however, was not only against allegations of child abuse. It was also against the social construction of motherhood. Yes, in the eyes of this woman (more than likely a mother herself) I was a 'bad' mother, an out of control mother with an out of control child. 'Good' mothers do not lock their children into the boot of the car. 'Good' mothers do not have children who bite them or who try to run away from them. I had, like many other mothers-to-be, read manuals on childrearing preparing for the event of having a child. I was never ever going to lay a finger on my child, as I did not believe in corporal punishment. And here I was, a mother-of-two, reported to the police for child abuse.

Four years later the situation was reversed. My now 11-year-old boy, tall and handsome, beat me up in a car park. I had prevented him from banging our car door into another parked car where a man was sleeping. I pulled him out of our car, locked it quickly and ran. Furious over having been physically restrained my son caught up with me, pulled my hair and beat my head and back with his fists. A horror-struck woman passed by in her car, pulled down her window and shouted 'If you don't stop hitting your mother like that I will call the guards!' He stopped immediately. My daughter, who had picked up my handbag and watched the incident from a distance, began to sob. The woman continued 'I have five children of my own, and I have never seen anything like this before!' I turned to my son and said 'Do you hear that now!' and he nodded quietly. The woman drove away and we continued doing whatever we had intended to do. I was glad she intervened as it had a dramatic effect on my son. But I was also furious at her statement 'I have five children'. Did that make her a better mother than I was? Was it her 'good' mothering that prevented her from being attacked by her children? Was it my fault that my child misbehaved like this?

As a mother of a child with autism, epilepsy and a mild learning disability I isolate myself deliberately from the world of mothers of non-disabled children. I find more support and encouragement from the mothers living in the same world as me. We mother our children with the same love and affection as any other mother does. We consider ourselves as good or as bad as anybody else regarding the way we mother. Many times we consider other people ignorant and judgemental and most of all totally unaware of what it really is like to mother a child with special needs.

This research was borne out of my experience of sharing my mothering dilemmas with other women in similar circumstances. There were so many stories told, so many questions asked and so many answers requested. But as this took place in a private and confidential setting, few people in the outside world would hear our stories. Thus, my commitment while beginning the research was to make these voices public. While my own personal story does not appear in this book, with the exception of this prologue, my voice can still be heard in the narratives of these women. My own journey with my son runs parallel with my participants' journeys. As they have had their ups and downs during the course of the study, so have I. My notebooks are filled with a mixture of their stories and mine. Research notes on one page, notes from a multi-disciplinary team meeting on another. While I was doing the fieldwork and interviewing mothers from all over the country, I was also involved in legal proceedings against the Department of Education, which culminated in the High Court. During my son's short life I have dealt with twelve psychologists, six psychiatrists, seven speech therapists, three social workers and numerous teachers, tutors, home support workers and special needs assistants. Despite this army of professionals he still ends up being suspended from his special needs school and sent back home to me – the mother, who is expected to do the job nobody else can manage.

My own personal experience has informed and shaped this research and has given me a passionate and political commitment to change the situation, not only for me but for all mothers living with special needs children in Ireland. My voice can clearly be heard among the voices of my participants and I believe that they also speak on behalf of thousands of other women in similar situations.

Chapter 1

Introduction

> I sometimes see myself as an arrow or a thorn. You don't start that way. I just wanted to be a mother. I wasn't aiming at anything.
>
> (Musgrave 2001)

The woman quoted above is Kathy Sinnott. Her comment was made in the context of her legal action against the Irish state on behalf of her adult son Jamie, diagnosed with autism. Although the media focus was mainly on Sinnott as a public campaigner, it also gave glimpses of the different maternal journey she was experiencing. The life-changing event of having a child with special needs had forced Kathy Sinnott out of her private sphere at home and into the public spotlight as she struggled for services and support. This book invites the reader to come along on this different maternal journey through the narratives of 18 mothers of children with Autistic Spectrum Disorder (ASD), Attention Deficit Hyperactivity Disorder (ADHD) and/or Down syndrome. Their stories form the core of the book, set in the context of contemporary Ireland. However, as this book will reveal, these maternal journeys are not unique to the Irish cultural and social context but echo similar maternal narratives in the Western world. Although various circumstances affect the lives of mothers differently, the commonalities are striking. Mothers of children with special needs, I will argue throughout this book, belong to a marginalized group of women, whose self-sacrifices are taken for granted. Their maternal work goes on unnoticed at home, neglected both culturally and financially by most governments around the world. More importantly, as the social construction of motherhood is deeply internalized, we follow narrow cultural scripts in our roles as mothers. To be a good mother, then, is to follow your natural instincts and just be there for your child. Mothering in reality, however, is not about simply being there, but involves constant activity. Few maternal experiences challenge the prevailing myth of motherhood as the experience of having a child with special needs. Mothering under these extraordinary circumstances makes it near to impossible for women just to be there, as the thinking and work intensifies.

Why mothers?

As I began researching for this book, an increasing number of mothers of children with special needs were making headlines in the Irish media. As a mother of a boy diagnosed with autism and a learning disability I could easily identify with these women who appeared in the news in the context of a 'struggle' or a 'war' against the state (see Prologue). They were ordinary mothers getting on with life in private until one day they felt forced to embark on a public struggle against the state. In the media they were described as tireless campaigners who fought for their children's rights with resilient determination. These conflicts created newspaper headlines such as: 'The mother of all battles…' (Musgrave 2001), 'Mother courage' (*Irish Examiner* 2001) and 'Taking action against a sea of State troubles' (*Irish Times* 2001a). Read (2000) has conceptualized this maternal challenge in her research involving British mothers of children with learning disabilities. She suggests that many of these women become their children's allies and are forced into a conflict with professionals, as there are little or no services available. As a consequence mothers become agents for their children and struggle for services despite very difficult circumstances in their day-to-day lives. Although this different maternal journey is shared by many women, the majority of these voices remain unheard. It was the invisibility of these women that prompted me to put their narratives centre-stage.

My decision to focus on mothers and exclude fathers was not made in order to undermine the role fathers play in families with special needs children. Mothers, however, are usually the primary caregivers and I have yet to come across research that would indicate the opposite. Similarly, during my years of personal involvement in parents' groups and organizations, both in my native country Sweden and in Ireland, I have met both mothers and fathers actively campaigning on behalf of their children. Yet I have never so far encountered a father who is both an advocate and a primary caregiver. This is usually the case for the mother who manages to do both. Thus my interest is predominantly the role of the mother and the maternal thinking and work (Ruddick 1989) invested in raising a child with a disability. Fathers are not excluded from performing this type of maternal work, although I would argue that it is relatively uncommon. As this book is written from a feminist perspective, I acknowledge and challenge the persistent gender divide that still exists between mothers and fathers. I argue that we have to be open about the differences between mothers' and fathers' experiences in the context of having a child with special needs. Why do we use the generic term 'parents' in scientific research on families, when the vast majority of research participants are in fact mothers? Many researchers are obviously aware of this misrepresentation, and add 'in particular mothers' after the word parents. It would, in my opinion, be more accurate to refer to mothers and 'some fathers' in the same context. Calling the mother a parent will not automatically encourage fathers to get involved in the maternal work, which so far is almost exclusively performed by mothers.

Gendered care work

Dalley, a feminist writer on caring, differentiates between 'caring for' and 'caring about' (1996, pp.13–14). 'Caring for' has to do with the physical task of helping another person, whereas the 'caring about' entails emotions. A mother is expected to do both, according to Dalley, and if she tries to separate the two concepts she is considered deviant.

> This blurring of the boundaries between functions typifies woman's universe. In the domestic sphere, the menial tasks of family servicing are wrapped up and presented as part and parcel of her role as a mother, and given the same affective values as the feelings she has for the family members for whom she is performing these tasks. (1996, p.14)

Having a child with a disability, a child whose dependency on the mother goes beyond what is normally expected, forces the mother to extend her affective links indefinitely. The large proportion of maternal time, in comparison to paternal time, spent with a child who is chronically ill, for example, is well documented (Dwyer Brust, Leonard and Sielaff 1992). Men, according to Dalley, do not have this complicated dual role and they can 'care about' without having to 'care for'. As far as men are concerned, to care about is to be 'responsible for' (1996, p.17) without having to do the actual tending. Thus the gender division of caring has consequences for official policies: women are natural carers (in the private and personal sphere) and men natural providers for care (which takes place in the public sphere).

Traustadottir discusses a third concept of care, 'the extended caring role' (1991, p.217), where mothers of children with disabilities extend their caring to other people with disabilities in general. Despite very difficult circumstances at home, in the day-to-day caring of the child and where the mothers are very limited in pursuing other roles, such as a professional career, many of them start advocating and campaigning in order to change existing services and policies. This is, according to Traustadottir, 'an extension of the mother's caring role and an expression of the mother's devotion to her child' (p.218). Second-wave feminists criticized this selfless mothering as a patriarchal trap for women (Chodorow 1978; de Beauvoir 1977; Firestone 2003). This criticism further marginalized women who for various reasons were full time mothers and carers, and contributed to a heated debate which positioned women against each other. The important question then is how feminists today can challenge the circumstances in which maternal work takes place, and at the same time empower the women who perform it?

Mothers as subjects

The last three decades have seen an increasing amount of feminist literature focusing on various aspects of motherhood/mothering (Bassin, Honey and Mahrer Kaplan 1994; Benn 1998; Kennedy 2002, 2004; Miller 2005; O'Reilly 2006; Ribbens 1994; Rich 1977). Rich (1977) challenged the patriarchal institution of motherhood and celebrated the maternal experience as something empowering. More recently, the diversity among mothers has been emphasized and calls to acknowledge factors such as race, class, sexuality and disability have increased (Abbey and O'Reilly 1998). Feminist writers have used a narrative approach to explore mothers as subjects in their own right, reflecting on themselves and their maternal thinking and practices. This has produced maternal counter-narratives and challenged existing myths around mothering (Malacrida 2003; Miller 2005). Motherhood then is often a challenging journey filled with disappointments and difficulties. For the majority of women, however, the reward is to see the helpless baby grow, learn new skills and eventually develop into an independent human being. All mothers and babies are different in their own ways, but most children follow a path of normal milestones and do things that are expected from them.

This book explores in depth the different maternal experience involving a child with special needs:

- What happens to a mother when her child does not follow an expected, normative path of development?

- How does she cope with a diagnosis of a learning disability and the demands of ordinary day-to-day life?
- What is it like to mother a child with special needs in today's modern high-tech society where we are bombarded with experts' advice on how to do the right thing?

Having a child with special needs, according to my own experience, drastically sent me into a new world where childcare manuals and well-meaning advice from family and friends became useless. In books written by experts such as Penelope Leach (Leach and Jessel 1997), the management of children with disabilities was reduced to being mentioned at the end of the book in the form of a referral to seek advice elsewhere. This symbolized the exclusion of these children and their mothers from mainstream society at an early stage of the child's development. This trend is beginning to change, however, as Leach's most recent book (Leach and Matthews 2003) contains many references to children with special needs throughout the book. As a Swedish mother living in Ireland, trying to find childcare for my infant son while pursuing an academic career, I was amazed by the lack of choices I had as there was no state-funded childcare here. Furthermore, when I entered into the 'world of special needs' I realized that the choices were virtually non-existent and that I had no choice but to become a full-time carer for my child.

As I embarked on this different maternal journey, I discovered fellow mothers who shared this experience with me. However, as I began to look for support in literature I was disappointed. There was already an abundance of literature on various childhood disabilities and learning disorders, written both by professionals and parents. Similarly, there was no lack of books on teaching methods, therapies, diets and other support for these children on the shelves in bookstores and libraries. In the majority of these books, however, the need of the mother was seldom raised; most topics related to how the child's quality of life could be improved. Nowhere could I find a book that shifted the focus from the child to the mother and explored how this maternal experience impacts on women's identities as individuals. While it is important to acknowledge the close relationship between the child's wellbeing and that of the mother's, there is also a need to enable mothers of children with special needs to recognize their own aspirations and needs for self-fulfilment. I was looking for a book that addressed issues such as society's images of the self-sacrificing mother and mother-blame, but in the context of raising a child with a learning disability. However, as the book I wanted to read did not exist, I set out to write it myself with the help of other mothers in similar situations.

Feminist ethnography

I chose to focus on learning disabilities and deliberately omitted physical disabilities in order to put a realistic boundary on this immense subject. As my personal experience is one of learning disabilities I also felt more comfortable researching that particular area. To further limit the study I decided to focus on Down syndrome, Autistic Spectrum Disorder and Attention Deficit Hyperactivity Disorder. These three disabilities are the most common and well known in the Western world and parents' support networks for these conditions are in place. I also limited the group of participants to mothers of children born between 1990 and 1992 for the purpose of focusing on primary school children. Therefore, mothers of very young children and of adolescents/adults were not included in the research. With these limitations I cannot claim to represent the experiences of all mothers of children with learning disabilities in Ireland, as the research findings are based on the narratives of a selective sample of women at a particular time in their lives. I adopted a feminist ethnography with its qualitative research techniques such as in-depth interviewing and a close researcher–researched relationship as a methodological approach. Emancipation, empowerment and reflexivity are key themes in this type of research and as a feminist my political agenda focuses on existing gender divisions within a patriarchal society. As a mother of a child with a learning disability I also describe my research as political and passionate, with the aim of challenging existing disability laws and policies.

My participating mothers were recruited through various disability organizations and support groups such as Down Syndrome Ireland, the Irish Association for Autism, the 11 member support groups of INCADDS (Irish National Council of ADHD/HKD Support Groups) and Aspire, the Asperger Syndrome Association in Ireland. The final sample group was a heterogeneous group coming from various socio-economic backgrounds. The average age of the women was 40 (ranging from 29 to 50 at the time of the first interview) and the average age of the children was 8.8. The participants lived in seven different counties, both in urban and rural settings. Fifteen were married and three were single at the time of the first interview. Twelve of the mothers worked at home full time and six worked outside the home, either full time or part time (see the profile of participants in the Appendix). The relationship between me and my participants commenced before the face-to-face meetings and was usually established after the first phone call. Some phone calls were lengthy, lasting over an hour, and much information was exchanged at that early stage. Time and place for the interview was decided, and I did my utmost to facilitate the mothers by meeting them where and when it would suit them best. Of the 18 interviews conducted, 16 took place in the participant's own home, mostly in the kitchen or the living room. Two interviews took place at night, in the lounge of my bed and breakfast accommodation or in the hotel room where I was staying at the time. When entering into someone's house I always felt very welcome and I was generously offered food and drink. My personal feeling was that there was a trustful relationship established almost immediately. During the course of the interviews I also told my own story, which I felt was appreciated and contributed to shape the interview to more of a dialogue than a researcher–researched situation. I wanted my participant to feel free to interrupt me and ask for clarification of questions and explanations and thereby avoid misunderstandings and misinterpretations. Likewise, I could follow up vague answers and in turn ask for clarifications.

I met with my participants twice and over a longer period of time, and gave the mothers an opportunity to comment both on my preliminary interpretations of the data as well as the research process itself. Many of the mothers felt supported by reading their own stories in the context of other mothers' voices. The research process then became an achievement in itself, as this shared consciousness was hugely affirming for many of the mothers. Several phone conversations with my participants throughout the research process and the follow-up meeting one year after the initial interview provided me with a good update on the current situation in which the mother and her child found themselves. In many cases it confirmed the constant transitions that these mothers made during a relatively short space of time. Instead of basing my research findings on a once-off meeting, however in-depth and long it might be, I now had an opportunity to correct misunderstandings from the first meeting: my perception of the single mother's lonely journey was in fact not true, the ex-partner, although never mentioned in the first interview, was very much part of the picture and an important support to the mother. Likewise, the apparently supportive husband, who was very good with the child from a practical 'hands-on' approach, tended to be less of a support on a more communicative level, thus leaving the mother feeling even more alone. Another reason why some new data was revealed during the follow-up process could be the less formal approach that I decided to take. I did not audiotape the second interview, and in my effort to thank my mothers for participating in the research, I treated them to a lunch/dinner, depending on circumstances. In some cases, where it was convenient and practical, I met with two participants at the same time, increasing the possibility for an exchange of views and ideas on the topic of mothering a child with special needs. This proved to be very successful and very much appreciated by the mothers. In some cases 'a night out' was a rare occasion for these hardworking women. I did not take notes during these conversations, as I wanted to be participating in the conversation and keeping eye contact with the mothers rather than looking down on notes. Nevertheless, if a certain comment was particularly relevant to the research, I wrote it down immediately, or else straight after returning home. These notes were selective and subjective; however, as fieldwork notes they were still of importance and relevance.

Many of my mothers said that they felt tired or shattered after the first interview, which is understandable. The experience after the follow-up meeting was completely different, perhaps more so for me. The image of an exhausted mother telling me of her struggle was still on my mind as I arrived for the second meeting. Perhaps that is why I was so pleasantly surprised to see the women again, in particular those dressed up for a night out. This positive image was reinforced by the tone of the conversation that followed, very strong and positive. Again it showed the importance of having more than one opportunity to meet with research participants in order to represent their voices.

Outline of chapters

Chapter 2 'The Challenge of Maternal Voices' provides a theoretical and historical framework for the narratives. It discusses existing research and literature on mothers, with an emphasis on feminist writings on motherhood/mothering. The second part summarizes policies and legislation on disability in Ireland. I also discuss how these policies have been challenged through landmark court cases taken by two mothers, Marie O'Donoghue and Kathy Sinnott. Finally, a comparative analysis is made between mothers' struggles in Ireland and in Sweden.

The mothers' constant fighting for services is emphasized in Chapter 3 'Maternal Coping'. This is discussed in the context of the themes of diagnosis, grief, stress and coping. The first part of the chapter relates to the mothers' experiences of getting a diagnosis for their children: how it happened, their own reaction to it and the way this information was handled by the professionals. The second part is devoted to the experience of living with a child with a learning disability. I discuss the core theme of coping and give examples of what the mothers find helpful to get on with their lives. The chapter also explores the main causes of stress and depression and how these experiences affect the mother's quality of life. An important part of this issue is the mothers' relationship with professionals and service providers.

Chapter 4 'Maternal Work and Employment' discusses the theme of the mother's employment and how a child with a learning disability impacts on her choice of occupation and her opportunities for personal fulfilment. Factors impacting on the mother's choices, in terms of a career and employment outside the home, versus staying at home full time, are discussed. I also analyse the issue of the 'maternal work' involved in mothering a child with special needs, where mothers provide training and education for their own children. Furthermore, these mothers spend much time and energy dealing with professionals and service providers for the purpose of helping their child.

The difference between mothers and fathers in the context of having a child with special needs is discussed throughout the book, but is explored in depth in Chapter 5: 'Mothers' Relationships with Fathers, Families and Social Networks'. Here, I move the gender discussion further and analyse the different roles mothers and fathers play in the lives of their children. The socially constructed role of 'good' versus 'bad' mothering is discussed, in particular how this 'mother-blaming' culture affects mothers' experiences in different ways. Another theme explored in this chapter is the theme of family life and how a child with special needs affects the whole family, including siblings. Finally, I discuss the mothers' experiences of the relationship with the extended family and society in general, including how they deal with moral and cultural prejudices regarding childhood disabilities in society.

The final chapter, Chapter 6, draws together themes and theories discussed throughout the book. It explores different ways of moving forward in order to support and empower mothers of children with learning disabilities, not only in Ireland but also elsewhere in the world. A good way to begin is to make the voices of these mothers heard.

Chapter 2

The Challenge of Maternal Voices

Voices of mothers of children with special needs are seldom represented in literature. This void is apparent both within scientific research on learning disabilities in general as well as in feminist writings on motherhood/mothering. This chapter takes a closer look at existing literature on mothers of children with special needs. I discuss how researchers have portrayed these mothers, and also how mothers themselves have documented this lived experience. The second part of the chapter focuses on maternal voices in the Irish context, in particular three mothers who brought their private concerns to the public and political arena.

The bulk of disability research on mothers of children with special needs consists of large-scale quantitative research mainly undertaken by psychiatrists or psychologists, using tools such as personality tests and questionnaires (Fitzgerald *et al.* 2000; Hoare *et al.* 1998; Joesch and Smith 1997; McGlinchey 2001; Olsson and Hwang 2003; Ryde-Brandt 1991; Veisson 1999; Warfield *et al.* 1999). Mothers are often found to be more stressed and depressed than fathers, but these statistical findings are seldom analysed in depth. Similarly, more family-focused qualitative research generally overlooks the mothering aspect in raising a child with special needs (Ainbinder *et al.* 1998; Baldwin and Carlisle 1994; Beresford *et al.* 1996; Case 2000; Dale 1996; Dowling and Dolan 2001; Grant and Ramcharan 2001; Knox *et al.* 2000; Murray 2000; Sloper 1999; Snell and Rosen 1997). Some researchers, however, have decided to focus solely on maternal narratives (Home 2002; Horgan 2004; Malacrida 2003; Read 2000; Redmond and Richardson 2003; Ryan 2005; Tarrant 2002; Todd and Jones 2003). Todd and Jones (2003) set out to research parents of adolescents with intellectual learning disabilities living across South Wales. The majority of these parents (30 out of 38), however, happened to be mothers and the authors decided to focus on the maternal data:

> This is not to marginalize the experiences of fathers but a recognition that it was typically mothers who had had a longer-standing participation with professionals. Furthermore, where fathers were reported to be equally or more involved in the day-to-day care of their disabled child, it was mothers who still seemed to have more contact with professionals. (Todd and Jones 2003, p.231)

Of particular interest is Todd and Jones's acknowledgement of the social construction of motherhood (p.242). The researchers discuss how the notion of 'good mothering' influences the self-perception of the mother and consequently her relationship with professionals. The participants in this research described themselves as advocates for their children first and foremost. They insisted that what they were doing was what any ordinary 'good' mother would do anyway. The narrators were, according to the researchers, also very reluctant to express their own needs, as they were afraid of being perceived by professionals as selfish. I will return to this self-silencing later on in this chapter.

The importance of giving a voice to mothers is also emphasized in an Australian study (Tarrant 2002), where the experience of fourteen mothers of children with autism is documented. As in other studies (Read 1991 and 2000), these mothers expressed their frustration with the lack of support in parenting a child with special needs and identified problems with diagnostic and educational services, unmet needs, widespread community ignorance and misinformed professionals. Tarrant calls her thesis *The Maternal Metamorphosis* to describe the evolving process of the participants' adjustments to living with a child with autism: despite hardship and struggle, the mothers' self-confidence increased and they learned to 'trust maternal intuition' (2002, p.80). This aspect of the mother of a child with a learning disability is seldom researched and rarely acknowledged as relevant. Tarrant is herself a mother of a teenage boy diagnosed with Asperger syndrome and she was therefore able to relate well to her research-participants' lived experiences. Home, a Canadian researcher, explored the lived experiences of 39 employed mothers of children with Attention Deficit Hyperactivity Disorder and argues that the oppression of mothers is the result of the persistent gender division of labour that still prevails in Canadian families. Women's unpaid family work remains undervalued and invisible, while the 'high economic, social and psychological costs borne by women go unrecognized' (2002, p.2). Home calls for action-research to promote social change and for social workers to join mothers 'in their struggle to move this issue higher on the public agenda' (p.8). This struggle is also often evident in texts written by people with disabilities, or by their families, and provides the most telling account of this particular life experience. There are many books and essays written by mothers of children with special needs all over the world, the majority of them presenting the story of a child with a particular learning disability and the mother's experience.[1] While some mothers give very personal accounts of their own lives, others tend to address issues such as the political context or the disability itself.

Irish mothers have been reluctant to go 'public' with private family matters and it is only in the last two years that literature on mothers as subjects has been published (Enright 2004; Kennedy 2004; Looney 2005). Even published Irish writers who are mothers of children with special needs have remained silent about their own personal lives and ambitions in their work. Through Annie Ryan's writings (I will return to her later in this chapter) we know everything about the Irish state's neglect of people with disabilities (1999), but nothing about what this depressing reality did to her as a person. Similarly, Ann Hewetson has documented other American writers' personal narratives (2002) and in a more recent book she also tells the story of her own son Mark who has Asperger syndrome (2005). Whereas this book gives a wonderful and detailed account of how she and her family struggled to understand Mark's condition and support him, she reveals almost nothing about herself and her own life.[2]

Mothering with a difference

Most existing academic contributions on mothers of children with special needs as subjects in their own right, originate from the US (Greenspan 1998; Kittay 1999; Landsman 1998; McDonnell 1991). Kittay (1999, 2002), an

---

1 Most support groups with websites (see Useful Contacts at the end of this book) provide reading lists. I also give examples of books written by mothers of children with special needs.

2 Liam Nolan, Irish broadcaster and writer and a father of a boy with autism, has written a book *Once in August Long Ago: A Week in the Life of an Autistic Boy* (2004). Nolan's book is an honest and personal account of having a son with autism. It portrays the experience of the father as a primary caregiver, albeit only during one week, in an excellent way.

American professor of philosophy, writes about her daughter who was born with a severe learning disability. Kittay criticizes liberal society's tendency to rely on goodwill and charity in providing care for its dependent citizens. She calls for a caring based on justice where dependence is positively acknowledged and met by a collective responsibility (2002, p.272). In this caring concept, society values both caretakers and caregivers and recognizes their rights as human beings. Kittay argues that although her daughter cannot 'pay back to society anything of material value' (2002, p.273) her contributions are nevertheless great: 'Watching her grow and develop skills and take part in her accomplishments nurtures me as much as my own work' (2002, p.273). Furthermore, Kittay and her husband wanted to pursue their professional careers, their parenting of their other child and their leisure activities, not only for their own sake, but also so they could keep loving their daughter without feeling resentful.

> We have moved to a model, which for want of any other adequate term I'll call 'distributed mothering'. I am Sesha's mother; but in truth her mothering has been distributed across a number of individuals: father, various caretakers and Peggy. (Kittay 1999, p.13)

Kittay challenges ideals on mothering in society, which focuses on fostering the independence of the child, a theme reflected in most feminist writings on motherhood. According to Kittay, a mother with a disabled child puts her heart and mind not so much to foster independence as to 'enable development' (1999, p.21). In order to realize this sense of accomplishment, the mother needs to know that what she is doing is the best she can do, which in turn means that she needs access to knowledge, financial, medical and educational resources. Kittay herself admits that she is very privileged to have the resources to pay a person like Peggy, an Irish nanny, who over the years became Sesha's second mother (1999, p.15). It is also interesting to note that Kittay considers herself lucky in comparison to mothers with, for example, children with autism, as she feels that Sesha is giving something back to her with her affection and love. Many children with autism would not be able to show this affection and, as most research has shown, mothers of children with autism do suffer more from stress and depression than mothers of children with other disabilities (Dumas *et al.* 1991; Sanders and Morgan 1997) and there is also more stigma attached to parenting a child with autism (Gray 1993).

McDonnell, an American mother of a boy with autism, has reclaimed 'the voice of the mother' (subtitle) against male experts who have blamed mothers for causing autism in their children. McDonnell refers to one of the 'chief experts' Bruno Bettelheim who claimed that autism was a child's defence against a rejecting mother (1991, p.58), a belief that became widespread in psychological and childcare literature and is still causing silence, guilt and pain among mothers of children with autism. Furthermore, McDonnell urges us to confront some of our cultural beliefs about good mothering and the mother-child relationship, and she argues that the deepest challenge for the mother herself is to 'reconstruct her subjectivity by reappraising some of her own deepest convictions' (p.60). A child with autism brings another reality to mothering, which McDonnell describes as sometimes 'unnervingly "other"' (p.65). Many children with autism become obsessed with objects, which in our world are only objects, but in their world mean something else. McDonnell's own high-functioning boy with autism was, at different stages, fascinated with light switches, screwdrivers, pipes, scales and thermometers: 'For the parent of the autistic child, such difference can be profoundly unsettling. Mothering, we all know, is in many ways a very normative activity' (p.65). McDonnell also discusses how some mothers, in the gaze of people in public, are tempted to punish their child for behaviours that would have passed unnoticed at home. She refers to Ruddick who sees this as betraying the child and calls it 'inauthenticity' (1989, p.109). Ruddick argues that the mother fails her child by losing confidence in her own values.

McDonnell brings this discussion further in the context of having a child with autism:

> If these are the temptations of mothering a normal child, what must they be for the mother of the autistic child who throws a tantrum in a public place because of some disturbing noise, who takes apart an unsuspecting neighbor's doorknobs and bicycles with a screw-driver, who screams when she hears the word 'cricket'? What is the mother to do in the face of such bizarrely different behavior. (1991, p.66)

The temptations to punish this child are, for this mother compared to Ruddick's mother of a non-disabled child, far worse. She might also choose to isolate herself from extended family, friends and neighbours, lose complete self-confidence and perhaps suffer great distress as a consequence. This sense of sole responsibility for the maternal work is a 'recipe for feeling inadequate' according to Greenspan (1998, p.42), an American mother of a girl with special needs. She argues that most mothers internalize a certain standard of mother care and suffer hardship and pain in order to fulfil society's expectations. This in itself creates a 'self-enforced silencing' (p.43) among these women who prefer to keep their pain and exhaustion private. Greenspan urges mothers to 'resist silencing, censoring, and "disappearing" ourselves for the sake of holding up the image of "good" mothering' (p.44).

Similarly, Malacrida, a Canadian mother of a girl diagnosed with Attention Deficit Disorder (ADD), highlights the dilemma mothers face in trying to do 'the right thing' while caring for their children. Her book, based on the narratives of 17 Canadian and 17 English mothers, describes this maternal engagement as a Foucauldian 'truth game' (2003, p.45) where the mothers back up their own claims of knowing their child's needs best. Malacrida, however, points out the limited success the mothers have in pursuing this truth game as they are seriously limited in their actions by factors such as economy, time and a sense of entitlement and assertiveness. She rightly argues that it is vital to let these mothers speak for themselves about what they know and how they experience this culture of ADD. Their stories become a counter-narrative to existing 'notions of mothers as needy, of children as troubled, and of professionals as knowing helpers' (p.243). By applying this (counter-)narrative approach, and analysing how mothers make sense of themselves and their actions, we can find striking similarities among women across the Western world. Late modern society is characterized by globalization and rapid economic changes, and cultural differences between mothers are likely to become less pronounced (Miller 2005). Irish mothers' narratives then will probably mirror maternal accounts from other societies around the world where existing story lines dictate what women can and cannot reveal about motherhood.

The challenge of maternal voices: the Irish context

Life in modern Ireland has changed dramatically since it became politically independent from its former colonizer Great Britain in 1922. The last 30 years have seen Irish society transformed from a poor agricultural society to the Celtic Tiger – one of the fastest growing high-tech economies in the world (EU Presidency 2004). Despite these changes, it still remains a patriarchal society with family legislation strongly influenced by the Roman Catholic ethos: contraceptives were illegal until 1979, divorce illegal until 1996 and abortion is still illegal after several referenda. Historically, the Roman Catholic Church endorsed the Irish state's principle of subsidiarity as a central element in service provision and family policy in Ireland, where family life was sacred and should not be interfered with by the state (Kiely and Richardson 1995). This was further reinforced in the Irish Constitution 1937:

1. In particular, the State recognises that by her life within the home, woman gives to the State a support without which the common good cannot be achieved.
2. The State shall, therefore, endeavour to ensure that mothers shall not be obliged by economic necessity to engage in labour to the neglect of their duties in the home. (Article 41, Section 2)

Article 41.2 has come under increased scrutiny during the last decade for being out of date. A government review group has recommended significant amendment to this article on the basis that it should be gender neutral (All-Party Oireachtas Committee on the Constitution 2005). Over 55 per cent of Irish women aged 15–64 now participate in the workforce (Central Statistics Office 2004a), a number nearly doubled since 1949 (Central Statistics Office 2000). However, in an international perspective, the figures still reflect the traditional status Irish full-time mothers have in the home. Over 73 per cent of Swedish women in the same age-group, for example, are engaged in employment (Statistics Sweden 2006).

Kennedy (2002) has emphasized the need for new and groundbreaking changes in Irish policies as more women combine careers with family life. She highlights many important dilemmas facing mothers, such as the lack of good quality and affordable childcare, job-sharing and flexitime. While services are thin on the ground for mothers of non-disabled children, services for mothers of children with special needs are virtually non-existent. In this sense, very little has changed regarding the perceived role of the mother in Irish society. A true Roman Catholic mother in post-colonial Ireland had as many children as God would give her, with church and state strongly supporting her morally in this role. Mothering was a duty, and one can imagine that the immediate needs such as food and clothes were always the priorities for the mother. The state took care of the basic education, for those who were able, but it was a different story for those children who did not fit into the system. In Article 42 of the Constitution the separate roles of the state and the family were outlined as far as education was concerned:

> The primary and natural educator of the child is the Family and [the State] guarantees to respect the inalienable right and duty of parents to

> provide, according to their means, for the religious and moral, intellectual, physical and social education of their children. (Section 1)

The state, in turn, 'shall provide for free primary education' as a 'guardian for the common good' (Article 42, Sections 3 and 4). Around the time of the writing of this constitution, a child named Christy Brown was excluded from the Irish state's 'free for all' education. He was born with cerebral palsy in 1932 and in his book *My Left Foot,* originally published in 1954, he pays tribute to his mother, who extended her 'duties' beyond feeding and washing, and fought tirelessly to ensure that he too, like his other non-disabled siblings, would have access to an education.

> Finding that the doctors could not help in any way beyond telling her not to place her trust in me, or, in other words, to forget I was a human creature, rather than to regard me as just something to be fed and washed and then put away again, mother decided there and then to take matters into her own hands. (Brown 1998, p.11)

Christy Brown wrote his book in 1950s Ireland, where the family was treated as the basic unit of social welfare and where the focus was on how to increase economic prosperity rather than social provisions (Conroy 1999). Brown was fortunate to be very talented intellectually and also to have an extraordinary mother. Anyone who has read Christy Brown's account of his mother's struggle, or who has seen the film based on the book, can see that Mrs Brown was the ideal Irish Roman Catholic wife and mother. Married to a bricklayer, she gave birth to 23 children, nursed and reared those who survived and sent them off into the world. What made her different was that she did not accept the 'experts' attitudes' regarding Christy, but made sure his full potential would be reached. It is not surprising that the first word he scribbled with his left foot, on the floor with a chalk, was 'Mother'. Four decades later, in 1975, Davoren Hanna was born in Dublin. His life resembled that of Christy Brown in many ways. They were both born with cerebral palsy and became famous Irish poets. Furthermore, Davoren's first written word was 'Mama', using magnetic plastic letters on a blackboard (Hanna 1996). Christy's and Davoren's mothers invested all their time and energy into working with their children. Others chose a more public approach by mobilizing people into action.

'Mother power': the rise of the disability movement

Annie Ryan, mother of a boy with autism and learning disability, experienced the Irish state's disregard for disabled children when her 12-year-old son had nowhere to go. Her frustration over the lack of services for the learning disabled in Ireland prompted her to write the book *Walls of Silence*, published in 1999. It describes the British legacy of mental hospitals, and how Ireland inherited these institutions built in early and middle Victorian times. In the early 1800s people with learning disabilities were either housed in these 'mental' hospitals, or in jails or industrial houses placed all around the country. In 1821 the Lunacy (Ireland) Act was passed, and most of the Irish mental hospitals were consequently built. Very early there was 'a group adrift' (Ryan 1999, p.22). These were the 'mental defectives', mainly children with behavioural problems (today they would probably be diagnosed with Autistic Spectrum Disorder). The psychiatric hospitals did not want them and as the demand for places for these children increased politicians discussed legislation. Annie Ryan's son Tom, born in the 1960s, belonged to the group of children for whom the state could not provide any service. He was dismissed from two special schools and spent five years in a school in Belfast where he was accepted. After a public protest and the formation of a parents' group, Tom was admitted to St Ita's, Portrane, a mental hospital in Dublin. Annie Ryan, however, did not give up her campaigning but fought tirelessly for reform of services for people with learning disabilities in the 1970s. She was president of NAMHI (National Association for Intellectually Disabled in Ireland) from 1992 to 1994 and received the Rose Fitzgerald Kennedy Mother's Award in 1998. Her book is dedicated to Tom 'who endures a difficult life with great courage and dignity' and confesses that had she not been his mother, the book would never have been written.

Thus, while successive Irish governments had failed people with learning disabilities, their families began to take things into their own hands. One such person was Patricia Farrell, mother of Brian, born in 1946 with Down syndrome. Farrell was ahead of her time in many ways and decided to widen her horizons in order to learn more about her son's disability. In 1955 she travelled to London where she met a parents' support group, and she returned to Dublin determined to start something similar here in Ireland. A committee was set up after the first public meeting and a year later, in 1956, the first day care centre for disabled children in the country was established. The association was called St Michael's House, and is today a very large service provider catering for people with many different types of disabilities and of all ages

(McCormack 1987). Patricia Farrell's initiative inspired parents all over Ireland to unite in their efforts to create day services for their children with disabilities. NAMHI, the National Association for Mentally Handicapped in Ireland (the term 'mentally handicapped' has now been replaced with 'intellectually disabled') was formed in 1962 and became the umbrella organization for these parents-and-friends' groups all over Ireland. NAMHI was renamed Inclusion Ireland in 2006, and today has over 72 member organizations actively campaigning on behalf of people with learning disabilities and their families and friends.

1980s: new efforts based on old thinking?

In the early 1980s the Irish government decided to review the situation, and issued *Education and Training for Severely and Mentally Handicapped Children in Ireland* (Department of Health 1983a), commonly known as 'The Blue Report' due to the colour of its cover. While the report acknowledged more progressive developments elsewhere, for example in the UK and the US where the right to an appropriate education for people with disability was enshrined in legislation (p.9), the language used to describe the Irish context was full of praise:

> The history of special education for mentally handicapped persons in Ireland can be seen as an evolution from custodial care for a selected few in County Homes and psychiatric hospitals to the sophisticated differentiation of needs that we have today. (p.18)

Annie Ryan's views were in stark contrast to that of the Report's Working Party. According to her the Working Party seemed oblivious to many of the problems still remaining. Although a recommendation was made not to admit more people with intellectual disabilities into psychiatric institutions, there were no suggestions as how to remove the existing 2,000 individuals from the institutions in the first place. Annie Ryan's objections, however, remained invisible in the produced report, as it contained no reservations whatsoever.

A Green Paper on services for disabled people, *Towards a Full Life*, was also published in 1983 and was full of aspirations. However, as a response to many calls from 'organisations and individuals' (Department of Health 1983b, p.112) to introduce rights-based legislation in Ireland, the report issued warnings:

> the most important thing which any disadvantaged minority needs is *goodwill and understanding* [my emphasis]. The Government are convinced that the promotion of the rights of disabled people can be best achieved by general agreement rather than by measures of compulsion. (p.112)

This patronizing statement was fully in line with existing policies of relying on the voluntary sector to provide services for people with disabilities, and by avoiding rights-based legislation the government could retain the status quo. The cost factor was important: the economy deteriorated in the 1980s and the country experienced high unemployment and mass emigration. Another deciding factor not to respond to calls for social reforms was that legislators and policy makers were reluctant to interfere too much in the private lives of the Irish people, a theme that was highlighted in the debate focusing on abortion, divorce and the rights of parents over their children. In the meantime, families of children with learning disabilities followed the traditional Irish pattern of giving a large input into voluntary organizations and formed different support groups. This relatively placid attitude, however, was about to change as mothers began fighting for their children in the Irish courts.

Landmark case 1: Marie O'Donoghue

The right to an education has not always been guaranteed for all Irish children, as already pointed out. For many years children with disabilities were excluded from the Irish educational system and it was not until the 1990s that the Irish state was confronted regarding this discrimination. This confrontation took the form of court cases against the state and the first landmark case began in 1991 when Marie O'Donoghue from Cork went to see a solicitor on behalf of her then seven-year-old son Paul who had a severe learning disability.

> From the time Paul was very young I had tried unsuccessfully to secure an education for him. However, all my letters, protests and lobbying were a waste of time because under the system that prevailed at the time Paul would never be able to go to school. As far as the State was concerned, children with severe and profound learning disabilities had no legal right to education. I was informed that Paul was the responsibility of the Department of Health who provide day care services but do not employ teachers. I wanted an education for Paul and believed he was entitled to it

> but, even had I been willing to accept day care facilities, without a teacher, there were none available. The best the state could offer Paul was to add his name to an already long waiting list for day services while at the same time admitting that they had no plans to create any of these services in the foreseeable future. (O'Donoghue undated)

Marie O'Donoghue's legal team put the case before the courts, arguing that under the Irish Constitution Paul had the same right to an education as all other children and that this education must be appropriate to his needs. The state, in failing to provide this education, was discriminating against Paul and depriving him of his constitutional rights. The case opened in the High Court in Dublin in June 1992 and continued over a three-week period.

> Counsel for the State were continuously suggesting that perhaps I was misguided in my faith in Paul's abilities and in my belief that Paul's needs could be properly described as 'primary education'. The State maintained at all times that children with severe and profound learning disabilities were 'in-educable' and the guarantee of free primary education of Article 42 of the Constitution did not apply to them. (O'Donoghue undated)

To support their arguments, Marie O'Donoghue's legal team produced evidence that education for this group of children had been compulsory in other European countries such as England, for many years, and also in the US. Furthermore, witnesses both from within Ireland and abroad stressed the importance of early intervention for these children. Ten months after the case was concluded, in May 1993, Mr Justice O'Hanlon ruled that the Minister for Health and the Minister for Education, in failing to provide free primary education for Paul and in discriminating against him as compared with other children, had deprived him of his constitutional rights under Article 42 of the Constitution (Naughton 1993). This judgment had far-reaching implications for both educational and health services in the provision of services to children with learning disabilities and the state feared huge costs. As a result the High Court Judgment was appealed to the Supreme Court in an attempt to have it overturned. It took another *five years* until the opening day of the Supreme Court hearing in February 1997. By this time, however, the state had understood that the outcome of a full hearing would not be to their benefit and the government was forced to withdraw. The following day, Irish national newspapers documented how 'a mother's battle for free education...forced the Government into a humiliating climb down that will cost it millions of pounds' (*Examiner* 1997). Marie O'Donoghue's concern was not limited to her own child, but in the aftermath of her victory she saw the need to inform other parents of children with learning disabilities that the law applied not only to Paul, but to every child with special educational needs. This hardline approach, I would argue, changed the scene regarding parents' actions on behalf of their children with learning disabilities. This was increased by a second landmark case which impacted dramatically on the disability movement in Ireland.

Landmark case 2: Kathy Sinnott

In October 2000 Kathy Sinnott, mother of Jamie, 23 years old and autistic, fought and won another battle in the High Court. The case established that the state had breached its constitutional obligation to provide Jamie with an appropriate education and, furthermore, that this education should be provided regardless of a person's age: 'Mother power wins over a deaf State – the 23-year campaign to secure primary education for Jamie Sinnott took its toll on a marriage, and on a family' (Carolan 2000).

Kathy Sinnott, a mother of nine living in Cork on her own (her estranged husband living elsewhere), told media reporters about her long and hard struggle to get appropriate services for her son Jamie. She recalled going back to her native Chicago for a short period and how Jamie, then in pre-school, had blossomed thanks to the services there. She fought in vain for the same education to be implemented for him in Ireland, and she claimed that she had no choice but to go to court. Kathy Sinnott recalled a psychiatrist in Cork advising her to put Jamie in an institution and concentrate on her two non-disabled children. Kathy, however, refused to give up and described herself as a former 'hands-on mother' who turned into a campaigner. Her victory, however, was short lived. The government decided yet again to appeal the High Court's decision. The main objection was against the argument that the constitutional entitlement to a free primary education is based on needs, not on age, and does not cease at age 18. Furthermore, the government also appealed the damages awarded to Kathy Sinnott. Some £55,000 of the total amount of £270,000 was awarded directly to Kathy Sinnott by the High Court, but the state only accepted to pay £15,000 of this amount (Carolan 2001). The government warned that 'the judgment creates dangerous constitutional precedents, because it awards damages for the first time to a person for the suffering of another' (Hennessy 2001).

Thus the focus of the debate switched temporarily from the child with special needs to the mother. The High Court judge had acknowledged and financially compensated Kathy Sinnott for her long struggle and personal sacrifices: 'A small, vivacious, almost painfully slim woman, it's easy to see why Mr Justice Barr declared that Kathryn "appears to have worn herself literally to the bone struggling on behalf of her son"' (Carolan 2000). Despite this acknowledgement the emphasis remained on the state's neglect of Jamie, the individual with a disability. No one mentioned the right of the mother to have a life of her own, but the portrayal of Kathy was that of the good mother who did all that was expected of her in order to fulfil that role regardless of the state's neglect.

In July 2001 the Supreme Court overturned the High Court ruling. The seven judges of the Supreme Court agreed that Jamie had not received the education he had been entitled to, but that this entitlement ends at the age of 18. Kathy Sinnott vowed to continue the fight despite the state 'abandoning' her son. In the aftermath of her case, the rights-based campaign for people with disabilities took a new dimension, in particular regarding the right to an appropriate education for people with autism. It was estimated that there were almost 200 legal actions being taken by parents with children with special needs throughout Ireland in the year following the Sinnott case (*Irish Times* 2001b). Kathy Sinnott was in the front line of this new campaign. She became patron of the newly formed Irish Autism Alliance, a pressure group fighting for the rights of people with autism and their families. Sinnott also ran as an independent candidate in the European Elections in June 2004 and won a seat in the EU parliament (Roche 2004). Starting off 'just wanting to be a mother' and ending up as a politician, Kathy Sinnott is an excellent example of a mother's extended caring (Traustadottir 1991). The Irish government, however, resisted disability campaigners despite international criticism.

Disability Bill: published and withdrawn

On 21 December 2001, the last working day before Christmas, the government published the long awaited Disability Bill. The overall reaction from disability groups was negative as it was not based on rights (NAMHI 2002). This led to a large protest rally in Dublin, where several hundred disability campaigners gathered together with politicians from opposition parties. As a consequence of these protests, the bill was withdrawn in March 2002 and the Minister, Mary Wallace, promised to invite the critics for further consultations. A second bill, the Education for People with Disabilities Bill was published on 22 March 2002, a few months before the general election. The aim was to make further provisions for the education of people with disabilities.

This bill also met with strong criticism as it included the government's right not to act upon the rights of the individual should the state lack the resources to do so. The bill's definition of a child was someone over the age of three, which angered advocates for early intervention. The Irish government was also criticized in an international perspective by independent social policy analyst and policy advisor in Dublin Dr Jane Pillinger who accused Ireland of being 'out of step with other international developments in disability rights' (Pillinger 2002, pp.1–2). Pillinger, drawing from EU based research focusing on quality services for people with disabilities, recommended 'a framework of improving service quality in respect of citizen, client or customer orientated services' (p.6) but acknowledged that this thinking was relatively new to Ireland (p.13).

The hypocrisy of the Special Olympics

As disability activists mobilized a strong action based campaign against poor services for people with disabilities, preparation for the 2003 Special Olympics World Games in Dublin in June were under way. The media coverage was extensive as 7,000 athletes with intellectual disabilities came to Ireland from all over the world. Brenda O'Gorman, mother of an eight-year-old girl with a learning disability, addressed a Kerry County Council meeting concerning the lack of respite services and noted that while she welcomed the Special Olympic athletes, she felt the funds should be spent on the disabled in Ireland:

> For the first four years of her child Carol's life, Ms O'Gorman said she was isolated from the outside world... 'No one could give me what I needed most, "a break"; not to go socialising, just time to be a parent to my other three children, who were very young at the time... As a mother my goal is to be the voice for my daughter. A voice that's going to be heard. I intend to fight for her right to independent living.' (Lucey 2003)

Donal Toolan, a member of the Disability Legislation Consultation Group, sharply criticized the Irish government's failure to legislate for people with disabilities and the hypocrisy of hosting 2003 Special Olympic festivities: 'The very word "rights" seems to send some Ministers into near hysteria, such is their disdain for what they call "human rights speak"' (Toolan 2003) Under a similar headline 'Hypocrisy behind the hype' Annie Ryan (see earlier in this chapter) once again spoke to an *Irish Times* reporter about her lifelong crusade for reforms in the Irish legislation for people with disabilities.

> There would be 'no big deal' about these rights. It would mean people would have their needs assessed and services would be tailored accordingly. This, she [Annie Ryan] and others maintain, would lead to better targeting of resources and improved structures. (Haughey 2003)

Halfway through the week of the Olympic games, the *Irish Examiner* published a photograph of Taoiseach (Prime Minister) Bertie Ahern hugging an athlete in front of the Special Olympic banner. Three questions were written into the picture:

> Taoiseach, if you support the Special Olympians then... Why are you spending millions in taxpayers' money, forcing the parents of children with intellectual disability to go to court for basic education rights? Why is the Minister for Justice Michael McDowell accusing parents of wasting resources by going to court for the very rights they are being denied? Why are you refusing to commit the Government to disability legislation, which would give disabled people legally enforceable rights? (Sheahan 2003)

According to this article, the government had spent 'well in excess of €10 million fighting parents seeking education for their children with special needs in the courts in recent years' and parents would have to continue to go to court unless the government delivered appropriate services.

Ireland in the international context

Ireland has also been the focus of criticism from both the EU and the UN for its lack of commitment to conventions on human rights. In April 2002 a special delegation under NAMHI went to Geneva to raise concerns with the United Nations Committee on Economic, Social and Cultural Rights, again protesting against the appalling conditions people with learning disabilities have to live under in Ireland (O'Morain 2002). Annie Ryan was one of them. The UN committee, following this protest, slammed the Irish government's treatment of people with disabilities (Shanahan 2002). The sharp criticism focused on the lack of a human rights-based approach in the government's proposed Disability Bill. The same committee had recommended Ireland to introduce such legislation three years previously. Furthermore, the committee also remarked on the large number of people with intellectual disabilities still living in psychiatric hospitals (*NAMHI News* 2002). Amnesty International, in a campaign unveiling the deficiencies of the Irish mental health system, also accused the government of leaving, among others, people with intellectual disabilities in inappropriate psychiatric institutions (Amnesty International 2002). In February 2004 a report revealed that only 25 per cent of services for people with physical and intellectual disabilities were meeting the standards set by the Department of Health. These figures were taken from a pilot project in a study commissioned by the National Disability Authority for the purpose of developing a basic set of mandatory standards (O'Brien 2004). In a separate article on the same page, beneath a photograph of a smiling Annie Ryan, reporter Carl O'Brien described her delight to see her son Tom moving from the psychiatric hospital of St Ita's in Dublin into a residential centre.

> The difference in the behaviour of her son since his move has been remarkable. 'There were times when he was utterly miserable, even though there were some very, very good nurses where he was. It was the system that was at fault. The difference is huge – it's not necessarily a difference of money. I wouldn't be surprised to find that it's cheaper than the old place. The difference now is that he has his own place. He's delighted now.' (O'Brien 2004)

Tom Ryan had finally – after more than three decades – moved into suitable accommodation. His mother Annie Ryan's lifelong struggle had finally paid off. But nowhere in all this did anyone ask about her own life and not once did she herself mention her own needs or rights as a human being – her identity is first and foremost as the mother of Tom. This is yet again a reflection of the image of the unselfish mother whose concern is always that of her child. Annie Ryan made a conscious decision not to reveal her private experience of mothering a child with autism in her book. She had 'strong objections' to writing about her son Tom, who was not able to give his consent, and she also considered the privacy of other family members. The most important thing to her was to reveal the history of the Irish state's neglect of people with disabilities.

Nevertheless, she acknowledges that a mother's work and worries culturally belong to the 'private' sphere in Ireland, whereas fathers are expected to be out in the 'public' (phone conversation with Annie Ryan, 1 June 2004). She recalls being told by a friend of her father not to be 'letting your family down' as she embarked on public protests over the appalling conditions in St Ita's, Portrane, in 1976. Another important decision that had to be made was whether or not Tom could continue to live at home with the rest of the family. Due to his disability the family life was disrupted and they could not sleep at night.[3] A residential place in a school in Belfast was available, and Tom went there at the age of seven. Annie Ryan and her family made this choice in order for the rest of the family to function and for Annie Ryan to keep up her job as a teacher: 'But we always told him we would never abandon him and we never did' (phone conversation with Annie Ryan, 2004).

Rights-based legislation: Sweden one step ahead

The mother of Fred – Maud Deckmar – has many things in common with Annie Ryan. Fred was born in Sweden in 1975 with autism and a severe learning disability. Maud Deckmar has written a book about her experience called *My Son Fred – Living with Autism* (2005). This book is about a mother's struggle to find help and appropriate services for a child with special needs. It is a personal account of the pain and hardship Maud and her family suffered during the years and it is written with the hope of supporting and comforting other families in the same situation. There is one important difference between Maud Deckmar's and Annie Ryan's books. Whereas Annie Ryan's book ends with a sense of hopelessness (her son Tom is kept in a psychiatric institution totally inappropriate to his needs), Maud Deckmar's son lives in his own apartment with 24-hour-support. Fred was nearly 18 when he moved into this purpose-built house with his own bedroom, bathroom, kitchen and living room. He had already been living part time away from his family in a group home for almost ten years, but Maud felt that this group home was inadequate due to the lack of space. In this new apartment, Fred could live as independently as possible but with the assistance of staff. He had his own front door with his name on it and a key to the lock. His family could come and visit – and tell the staff that no help was needed during this time. Maud sewed and put up curtains in Fred's apartment, baked bread and did things for her son that were probably very similar to what mothers do for their non-disabled children who leave home in their late teens.

Like Annie Ryan, Maud Deckmar had been actively involved in disability organizations and joined various planning groups within the county council. She kept working part time, but was on the verge of collapsing many times due to the combined pressure of caring for her son Fred and fighting against professionals, service providers and at times also the wider community

3 Prime Time's documentary on families living with autism in Ireland today (RTE 1, 10 May 2004) brought back memories to Annie Ryan who could identify with many of the families appearing in this programme.

(during the planning process of Fred's new house neighbours objected and put a temporary halt to the building). Maud documents the feeling of losing herself in the middle of all this: 'would it suddenly be enough to be just myself? I had forgotten how to be Maud. I only knew how to be Fred's mummy' (Deckmar 2005, p.133). Maud's decision to start living her own life again was very painful as it meant that Fred had to leave home permanently: 'The decision nearly killed me. I had to reach the bottom and nearly die before I could give myself permission not to cope' (p.142). Maud, a Swedish mother of a child with special needs, had done all in her power to fulfil the role of the perfect mother prepared to give her life for her son. When she eventually gave up, there was an alternative. The quality of the care provided for Fred was of a high standard and gave him a life worthy of dignity. Maud had to fight for it and acknowledged towards the end of the book that she was worried about the future: 'The future is scaring me now. All the talk is of reorganization and lack of funds. What will happen if Fred can't keep the staff and the apartment he has today?' (p.188).

It would be misleading to portray all Swedish services as as good as Fred's. A Swedish television documentary portrayed the appalling situation of Helene Sörensson, who had to walk with her daughter Nathalie on the suburban streets of Trelleborg in the middle of the night in order to let the rest of the family and the neighbours sleep (TV4 'Kalla Fakta', November 2002). Judging by many readers' letters to the Swedish Association for Autism's newsletter (*Ögonblick*) the situation for many families living with autism in Sweden are far from satisfying. Although there is rights-based legislation in place, only those who are able to take on the fight against local authorities and service providers benefit from legislation. One of them, Katharina Höglund, mother of seven-year-old Simon, autistic and severely learning disabled, had to fight hard in order to get appropriate care for her son. Not until then was she able to start thinking of her other two children and herself and return to her work as a nurse, something she was looking forward to. But this was only possible to pursue due to existing Swedish law (Persson 2004).

In addition to the general disability legislation in Sweden, a law specifically addressing the needs of people with certain disabilities, including autism, was introduced in 1993. 'Lagen om Stöd och Service till vissa funktionshindrade', LSS for short, is a rights-based law aimed to help individuals with certain disabilities when existing disability legislation is not enough. LSS entitles the individual to live a life as normal as possible and states that all measures should be taken to fulfil that aim. Included in these measures are, for example, access to professional help and advice, personal assistance, home help, short-term respite and residential care. The individual is also entitled to have an individual plan where the needs are assessed and how they are best met is considered. The individual (or his/her advocates) is part of creating this plan and service providers are responsible for putting the plan into action. In order to take advantage of services granted through LSS the individual has to apply for them. The local authority has the ultimate responsibility to inform the individual regarding these rights and to enforce them according to demand. If the individual is not happy with whatever services are offered, he or she can go to court. Swedish legislators have, through LSS , also acknowledged the right of the individual's family to live a life as normal as possible and not to be isolated and marginalized due to one family member's disability. One important section of LSS is the legal entitlement to financial compensation for personal assistance for the individual with a disability. This compensation can be paid out to any individual not older than 65 who has a need for this assistance averaging 20 hours per week. The needed assistance could be to help the individual with personal hygiene, feeding and dressing or, for the more high-functioning person, to participate in society through work or leisure activities. It is up to the individual to make the choice whether to use the local authorities' services or to employ an assistant privately. The individual cannot directly employ an assistant, but has to go through an independent organization/company. This has resulted in many new companies being formed solely for the purpose of providing assistants to families living with a disability. With the help of the law, many parents can be employed and paid by these companies in order to work as assistants for their own children and at the same time have backup from other assistants who are trained to work with these individuals (Assistansia, see www.assistansia.se). Another direct result of this legislation is a respite and residential service provider for people with autism, Enigma Omsorg (see www.enigmaomsorg.se), initiated and run by parents in the greater Stockholm area.

More than ten years after the introduction of LSS Swedish disability activists are critical of the local authorities' avoidance of implementing the law. Eva Nordin-Olson, a mother of a young woman with autism and chairperson of Autism Sweden, expresses her worries about the future in her editorial column in the organization's quarterly magazine *Ögonblick* (my translation):

> Many of us feel far from satisfied today. Many of us even feel betrayed. Some things are very, very wrong. Society says one thing, but does some-

> thing completely different. The local authorities are blaming the state, the state is blaming the local authorities. Some people openly question if we can afford LSS! (Nordin-Olson 2004)

Thus, the struggle for appropriate services for people with disabilities is not confined to Ireland, but appears to be universal. The UK, from which Ireland has inherited a lot of services and practices, as already mentioned, is no exception. As with Ireland, there is no single rights-based disability legislation in the UK. There are, however, different laws (Read and Clements 2001) that can be used as a tool in fighting for appropriate services for people with disabilities.

Mothers, then, are forced to go through the courts in order to obtain what should be offered as a matter of right. This additional stressful experience is an example of how society disables the individual instead of providing services that are supportive. One example is Tessa Woods, mother of Darren, nine years old and severely learning disabled, who won a landmark case for her son against the Irish state in March 2004. Tessa Woods wanted adequate support to care for Darren at home and a settlement was reached in the High Court. The case was primarily based on the European Convention of Human Rights relating to 'the right of life, to bodily integrity, to education and prohibiting inhuman and degrading treatment' (Carolan 2004). A similar court case was fought by Ann Mulligan, mother of 22-year-old Robert who has severe cerebral palsy, epilepsy, scoliosis and a jaundice-like condition called Gilbert's syndrome (Holland 2004a). Ann Mulligan took the South Western Area health board to the High Court in order to receive 24-hour nursing care for Robert at home. She wanted her son to remain at home full time, but due to the severity of his disability, she needed much more help from the state. The local health board, however, wants Robert in community care part time, and has threatened the mother to make him a ward of court. The mother, who has cared for her son at home with very little support for 22 years, is now accused of not acting in his best interest (Holland 2004b). This is yet again an example of the risks involved for a mother who breaks the silence and brings her private concerns to the public arena. She needs to have the law on her side in order to be empowered and supported on her maternal journey.

The Disability Act 2005: another fundamental flaw?

On 21 September 2004, over two years after the public had rejected the Disability Bill 2001, the Irish government published a new Disability Bill in the context of a National Disability Strategy. The main difference between this Bill and the rejected Bill was that the new Bill provided for the right to an individual independent assessment of needs and the right to redress and appeal. Karen Canning, mother of a 15-year-old boy with a severe learning disability and PRO of the National Parents' and Siblings' Alliance, had reservations about the Bill. The right to services, in her opinion, would not follow on from the right to an assessment, as resource constraints would determine levels of service provision. Canning had been a member of the Disability Legislation Consultation Group (DLCG) and she did not hold out much hope for families like hers: 'There are many parents in this country caring for their disabled children who are in their 40s and 50s. What kind of life do they have? What kind of life can we hope for in the future? Does this Bill offer us hope?' (Canning 2004).

Similar criticism against the Bill was made shortly after its publication, during a conference on disability and human rights in Galway. Legal experts and disability campaigners argued that the proposed legislation did little to guarantee the necessary funding on a sustained basis. Furthermore, the proposed appeals process included an infrastructure of assessment officers, liaison officers, complaint officers and appeals officers: 'an administrative game of snakes and ladders dressed up as an independent complaints system is no alternative to the vindication of rights by an independent and impartial court' (Coulter 2004). Despite this criticism the Bill was passed and enacted upon shortly afterwards and it remains to be seen how people with disabilities and their families will benefit from this new legislation (Disability Act 2005). As the Celtic Tiger continues to generate unprecedented wealth for Irish society, better services and support are demanded and anticipated by disability groups. As Ireland is catching up economically with other countries in the Western world, the problems facing mothers of children with special needs will become even more universal and increasingly reflect moral and cultural dilemmas rather than practical and political.

Conclusion

Theorizing motherhood is not a new phenomenon and calls to acknowledge factors such as race, class, sexuality and disability in such research are increasing. Mothering children with special needs, however, seems to be absent in the vast majority of feminist literature. Similarly, the bulk of disability research on mothers of children with special needs consists of large-scale quantitative research where the cultural context of the mothers is of little or no interest to the researcher. This research approach is dominated by a top-down relationship between professionals and mothers with a disregard to gender divisions. Mothers are found to be more stressed and depressed than fathers, but these statistical findings are seldom analysed in depth.

Many mothers of children with special needs have documented their personal experiences of this different maternal journey. These women are, however, predominantly American, as I have shown in this chapter. Two Irish mothers (Ryan 1999 and Hewetson 2002, 2005) who have written books relating to their children's learning disabilities do not reveal any personal information about themselves. This reluctance to go 'public', I would argue, may have its roots in the Irish culture of keeping family matters private. The strong Catholic ethos that influenced the 1937 Irish Constitution had long-lived consequences for Irish women in their roles as carers and homemakers. This socially constructed role of motherhood left mothers of children with learning disabilities alone and unsupported at home with little or no support from the state. Nevertheless, some of these women came together in groups as early as the 1950s in order to improve conditions for their children. Two landmark court cases, taken by Marie O'Donoghue and Kathy Sinnott, during the 1990s and early 2000s had further dramatic effects on the disability movement's campaigning tactics in Ireland.

Paradoxically, as I have shown through examples from Sweden, rights-based legislation does not automatically ensure that quality services for people with disabilities are implemented without a struggle. On the contrary, mothers in Sweden have to embark on the long and hard road of fighting for services the same way that their Irish peers do. This maternal struggle seems to take place regardless of social and cultural contexts and appears to be common amongst many mothers in the Western world. The next three chapters will focus on the narratives of 18 mothers and follow close-up this different maternal journey.

Chapter 3

Maternal Coping

> I felt like I was getting to the end of my rope, but when you get there you think, OK, I can go on a little longer, and it's like you push yourself or... You look at them and they're sleeping, and it's like, OK, I can do this a little bit longer...every time you get through something it gives you the encouragement to go through what's next.
>
> (Brenda, mother of Susan and Sally)

The core theme of coping, as it emerged from the mothers' narratives, is the focus of this chapter. The first part relates to the mothers' experiences of getting a diagnosis for their children: how it happened, their own reaction to it and the way this information was handled by the professionals. I begin with the stories of the mothers of children with Down syndrome, as they are diagnosed at birth. We move on to discuss the stories of mothers of children with autism and moderate to severe learning disabilities diagnosed at an early age. I will finally explore the stories of mothers of children with Attention Deficit Hyperactivity Disorder (ADHD) and Asperger syndrome, as these are usually not diagnosed until a child starts school.

The second part of the chapter is devoted to the experience of living with a child with a learning disability. I discuss the themes of grief, coping, stress and depression, and give examples of what the mothers find helpful to get on with their lives. The chapter also explores the main causes of stress and depression and how these experiences affect the mother's quality of life. An important part of this framework is the mothers' relationship with professionals and service providers.

Knowing from the beginning: Down syndrome

Down syndrome is one of the most common syndromes associated with a learning disability and was also the first to be identified as a syndrome. In 1866 Dr John Langdon Down gave name to this syndrome after publishing the first complete physical description of Down syndrome and showing how similar facial features affected people with this condition. After nearly another hundred years, in 1959, researchers discovered the cause behind the syndrome, an additional chromosome (21), and this condition was consequently named Trisomy 21. Some 95 per cent of children born with Down syndrome would be diagnosed with Trisomy 21, but there are two other types of Down syndrome, also caused by a chromosomal abnormality. These are Translocation (which accounts for 4 per cent) and Mosaicism (1 per cent). Children with Mosaic Down syndrome would score higher on IQ tests and would have fewer medical problems compared to children with Trisomy 21 and Translocation (Roizen 1997). Research in the US (Roizen 1997) shows a decreased prevalence of Down syndrome births from 1.33 per 1,000 to 0.92 per 1,000 since the 1970s. The decrease is explained as a result of the availability of amniocentesis, with many women opting to have an abortion if the foetus is identified with Down syndrome. In Ireland, where abortion is illegal, the prevalence is higher. The Eastern Regional Health Authority keeps a registry on congenital anomalies, which showed an incidence of 1.96 per 1,000 during the years 1980–99. Because of the physical features of a Down syndrome baby, a diagnosis is made relatively soon after birth. Some children with Down syndrome have behaviour and psychiatric disorders and Down syndrome could co-exist with ADHD or autism. Cahill and Glidden challenge research suggesting that children with Down syndrome would generally be easier to rear than children with other disabilities: 'False expectations of a positive nature can lead to self-blame and feelings of failure, as dangerous as negative expectations leading to a self-fulfilling prophecy' (1996, p.157).

The four mothers of boys with Down syndrome in this book all gave different contexts surrounding the birth of their children. In three of the cases the context itself was negative: one mother gave birth to her child a few hours after her own mother died, another mother had her child on a date associated with the death of a close relative and the third mother had a very difficult and painful delivery. These negative circumstances appeared to have affected the mothers' ability to cope with the news. Nevertheless, the knowledge of having a child with Down syndrome evoked similar emotional responses in these women. They confirm the initial shock and the grief that follows, but also the need to nurture this life that has just been born and carry on life as normally as possible: 'It's a very difficult thing, because it's, yes, it is terrible. But at the same time, here's this little life, you know' (Miriam). 'I was crying all the time...the two words Down syndrome used to go over and over in my head at night' (Margaret). The manner in which the professionals broke the news to the mothers seemed an important factor in how they experienced the situation. Miriam thought she saw features of Down syndrome in her son's face immediately after he was born and asked a junior nurse, 'It's Down syndrome, isn't it?' The nurse replied 'I'm not supposed to say anything, what shall I do now?' According to the hospital's hierarchal rules, this was the paediatrician's job, and he subsequently arrived with the matron of the small, private hospital. In the meantime Miriam asked the nurse to bring her baby in to her:

> [The paediatrician] was quite a dire person, the only positive thing he had to say was that 'they were very quiet children'. And I sort of looked at [husband] and I sort of said 'Well, that'll be a change anyway...because our first child especially had been a very lively child...and I remember I actually dismissed everybody in the end... I felt I was in charge of the situation and like 'go on now, you can all go now!' (Miriam, mother of William)

In Miriam's case the compassion of the matron was a great support, the way she came in for short conversations 'saying the right things at the right times'. One of these things was that Miriam was grieving for what she should have had, but that she still had something, and she had to go forward from there, 'so that made a lot of sense to me'.

In the second situation, Helen praised the way her paediatrician told her about Andrew having Down syndrome. Despite the circumstances (Helen's mother had died a couple of hours earlier in a different hospital) she felt that his words of comfort helped both her and her husband enormously.

> 'In simple terms' he said 'do you know anything about Down syndrome?' and we said no. He said 'basically, what it means is he'll do all the other things other boys do...he'll just be a bit slower... I'm going to get some information to you, have a read about it, give me a list of questions, and I'll come back to you in three or four days and we'll have a chat about it.' (Helen, mother of Andrew)

Helen tells of her 'medical' reaction when she and her husband were presented with some written information on Down syndrome and started checking the baby for all the characteristic features:

> [A]nd we were looking at Andrew and saying, well, let's have a look at his feet, just have a look at his hands, look at his eyes, and you're like inspecting this baby instead of...at no stage, I don't think, did it [the diagnosis] affect how I felt about Andrew. To me he just needed to be hugged and kissed and fed and changed and all the rest of it. (Helen, mother of Andrew)

In the third situation Betty, who had gone through a traumatic birth with a lot of haemorrhaging, was convinced her baby had been brain damaged as a result. This fear was heightened by the fact that the child had been taken away from her immediately and she had to go and look for him. A nurse, again obviously told not to break the news to this mother, took Michael out of the incubator and held him up.

> 'Look at him, what do you think is wrong? Have a good look at him, think about it, what do you think is wrong?' and I said 'Has he brain damage?' And she said 'no', but she still didn't say anything to me, I can never forget, I'll always remember the way she said it to me 'Look at him, think about it, what would you say?' (Betty, mother of Michael)

Betty was left wondering what was wrong with her child, until she was called into the office together with her husband. The paediatrician subsequently informed them that she was 95 per cent certain that Michael had Down syndrome:

> At that stage I thought the room was caving in on me... I forgot about the pains and aches at that stage, I forgot about the bad birth...so we were asked had we got any questions, and I said there were millions of questions but I didn't know...you know, I was so confused and mixed up and whatever...and I was handed a book immediately 'You and your Down syndrome Child' that I will never forget, it was way too soon, how they took the book off the shelf, this green book, I still have it and I can see it, the way it was written 'You and your Down syndrome Baby' and I thought, my God!' (Betty, mother of Michael)

The fourth mother, Margaret, held her baby for a little while, but he was taken away from her almost straightaway, as he was going blue:

> He was kind of whisked away then...and they put me into this empty ward, this huge, huge empty ward. They pushed the bed in there, there were no beds in there... I was on my own... I think my husband had gone up to the special care unit, had followed the baby up, so I was kind of on my own inside in this room, still kind of groggy after the birth, it was very shortly after the birth. (Margaret, mother of Jonathan)

Although the environment itself was depressing, Margaret experienced the paediatrician who broke the news to her as positive:

> I really just thought the baby was dead at that stage, you know, but then they, they told me. He was very good, now I have to say, he was very good, and he was very positive. I mean he talked about the positives, about, he didn't talk about what he couldn't do, he really spoke about other things he could do and I asked him questions, but I think really they were probably really stupid questions. (Margaret, mother of Jonathan)

In comparison to Miriam, Helen and Margaret, Betty was given the news about her baby without any warmth and compassion: 'she wasn't in any way warm, not by a long shot', and without the baby being present. The presence of the baby himself and a positive surrounding could have made a difference to Betty's reaction that day. She also acknowledged the fact that holding her child changed her own mind almost immediately.

> [B]efore I got him and fed him, I thought, if this child is going to be so sick, like, wouldn't it be better if God could take him away as a baby... and then I felt...I had a good feeling this fellow is going to survive and he's going to make it. I was very positive. (Betty, mother of Michael)

It is interesting to note that the mothers related their grief not to the newborn baby himself, but to worries about his future: 'I used to worry about his future all the time... I thought, God, what's going to happen to him when we're old, when we're gone...' (Margaret); 'part of the time I was in floods as well, thinking, How am I going to cope with the baby? You know, what is out there? What does the future hold?' (Helen). Another challenge for the mother was telling people about the diagnosis of the baby:

> I think for me it was...it must have been being brought up in the Irish convent...it was kind of what will all the neighbours think, when will I tell them, it was more *when* will I tell people. It was like this big

> compulsion, that you had to go out and tell everyone…it was this huge big struggle, do you tell everybody, or do you not tell everybody? And that took me a long while. (Miriam, mother of William)

The reluctance to talk about having a child with a difference reflects a culture that still stigmatizes children and people with disabilities (see Chapter 5 for further discussions on cultural issues). As time moved on, however, and the mothers went home with their newborn babies, they continued to live their lives as normally as possible. For all four mothers this baby was the third, so there was a household to run and siblings to be taken care of. And initially there were very few differences between these babies and others.

> [C]ertainly when he was a baby, anyway, there was no difference…and he was a very good natured baby…loved being passed around and smiling…and he was breastfed so that was no problem. (Miriam, mother of William)

> [W]hen you have a new baby in the house it's always kind of different, it's kind of a difficult time anyway, I suppose we had one bad fright, he was just discharged from the hospital, I think…he got a really bad attack and went really, really blue and we had to take him back to the hospital…and kind of after that he wasn't really a whole pile different to any other kid at that stage. (Margaret, mother of Jonathan)

These four mothers of children born with Down syndrome were in a situation where professionals immediately recognized the condition and there were certain support networks in place. On the other hand women, who give birth to what appear to be non-disabled babies often go through many years of worrying before they get any help.

Early years worries: moderate to severe learning disabilities

There is an image of the autistic child being locked into a glass cage with no contact with the outside world. It is very often said to be a beautiful child with unusually large eyes that avoid contact with other eyes. In the past, this autistic child must have been the 'changeling' in the Irish myth: the 'real' child was stolen by fairies and left behind was this 'inhuman' child, beautiful and healthy but completely blank inside (McDonnell 1991). In 1943 Dr Leo Kanner, an American child psychiatrist, identified a unique group of children who presented with similar behaviours. They failed to develop normal social relationships and they were upset by changes in the environments and had marked language impairments. Kanner called the condition 'early infantile autism' (Hewetson 2005, pp.51–3).

Three of the mothers contributing to this book had boys who showed signs of special needs within the first two to three years of their lives and who were later diagnosed autistic with a moderate to severe learning disability. In one case, Marie intuitively knew at a very early stage that there was something seriously wrong with her baby boy Eoin: 'He probably seemed the ideal baby, but I knew he wasn't. My heart sort of sank because I knew babies are meant to scream and scream and be hungry.' It took another nine months, when Eoin's weight was 'deplorable', before anybody listened to Marie's concerns. Although the medical side was taken care of, Marie was still frustrated over not getting any answers regarding his mental development:

> They never actually said to me he had a delay, and all I wanted was a direct 'yes he has a delay, yes, he is mentally handicapped'. Then I could get on with it, because I was grieving, a grieving nutcase at that stage, because I knew there was, but I had parents who were saying to me 'ah, for God's sake, you're being ridiculous', so I began to think I'm this nutcase who wants her baby to be delayed...but nobody would tell me. (Marie, mother of Eoin)

Eoin's diagnosis of a learning disability gradually went from mild to moderate to finally end up in a severe category. Marie describes herself being in a limbo for many years, looking at other children and comparing his development to theirs and knowing that he was disabled, but she was still shocked when she was 'officially' told.

> [W]hen I was given the severe diagnosis, one of the nurses...suggested that I was suffering a bit from depression, which I wasn't, I was just suffering from shock, grieving with shock, which was very natural. (Marie, mother of Eoin)

Many mothers of children with autism would say that a suspicion around the child's ability to hear is among the first signs that something is wrong. In Mary's case, however, she felt 'in the pit of my stomach that there was more to this than his hearing'. Another eye-opener for Mary was her second child, only a year younger than Patrick, 'only for doing that [comparing the two children] we would have lived in cloud cuckoo land for a little longer'. A year later Patrick also became very difficult to handle, with tantrums and head banging, and she was told by a psychologist that 'he tended to be more autistic than not'. The professional focus, however, was more on the severity of the learning disability than the autism. Patrick was Mary's first child, and she describes herself as a very carefree person prior to his birth: 'I suppose the fun in you dies in one way...you know...and it can die altogether if you let it.' Mary and Marie shared the experience of waiting for some time to get their own suspicions of a learning disability confirmed, knowing intuitively that there was a serious problem. Marie also expressed her frustration of not being told immediately. Caitriona had the opposite experience, being told bluntly by a doctor about her son Donnacha's probable autism and learning disability:

> I took him to the doctor at two and a half...even though not thinking there was anything wrong, but a bit suspicious in my own mind, I suppose, that something was a little amiss. So explained all my story to the doctor and he told me 'Yes, Mrs Murphy, you have cause for concern', he said, I mean I'll never forget the tone... 'your son either has autism or mental handicap or both'. (Caitriona, mother of Donnacha)

Caitriona did not really know what autism meant, and went home in 'a trance'. She also had serious marital problems at that time, and felt too exhausted to deal with her son's diagnosis immediately: 'I suppose it didn't affect me, I suppose like it would affect somebody who wasn't going through anything like that.' The paediatrician's suspicion of autism was confirmed through a psychological assessment where Donnacha was diagnosed as having autism and a learning disability, both at moderate levels. While these mothers were given a diagnosis relatively early in their children's lives, others had to wait longer.

After years of searching: the relief of a diagnosis

Attention Deficit Hyperactivity Disorder (ADHD) and Attention Deficit Disorder (ADD) are relatively newly diagnosed conditions and many children and adolescents are diagnosed late, some perhaps never. The procedures of diagnosis are difficult, as is the case with other psychiatric disorders. Exact causes of ADHD are unknown but the most probable cause is now thought to be genetic. Other causes would, for example, include premature birth with low weight, chromosome abnormalities and prenatal exposure to alcohol and drugs (Blum and Mercugliano 1997). ADHD, sometimes also called Hyperkinetic Disorder, is the most common neurological developmental disorder of childhood, affecting an estimated 5 per cent of school-age children, mostly boys. Children with ADHD are easily distracted, impulsive and hyperactive. They tend to have a low frustration tolerance, become bored easily and do not learn from previous mistakes (Blum and Mercugliano 1997). Parents and professionals are told to look out for children who have difficulties in following through instructions, who appear not to listen and who often lose things necessary for tasks and activities in school. Their impulsivity prevents them from turn taking in games, they intrude and interrupt others and blurt out answers to questions before they are completed. Thus they have problems making friends and they often engage in dangerous activities without thinking about consequences. If ADHD is left untreated, according to some professionals, the implications can be serious for the individual and lead to future criminal behaviour. This is particularly true for those children with ADHD who also have co-existing disorders such as Oppositional Defiant Disorder (ODD) and Conduct Disorder (CD) where delinquent behaviours such as aggression and rule-breaking are common (CHADD 2001).

Parents living with ADHD children are very often on the verge of breaking down. First, living with a child with this condition is in itself stressful and family life is difficult due to constant conflict and chaos. Second, the way society expects children to behave and fit in, further marginalizes these parents, especially mothers (Boethius and Rydlund 1998; Home 2002; Malacrida 2003). This is reflected in the language where 'He's a credit to you' is often heard or 'Give him a good slap, that'll sort him out'. With a hidden disability like ADHD it can also be hard to convince professionals that you are doing the best you can; the child just does not respond to 'ordinary' discipline. Medical treatment for ADHD has long been used in the US and has become common also in Europe. Ritalin, a stimulant medication, is the usual drug given to help children focus and concentrate and thereby enable them to follow through a full school day (Blum and Mercugliano 1997). The debate whether or not to use medication to treat ADHD and co-existing disorders has divided professionals and parents across the world. Malacrida (2003) argues that professional counterclaims concerning both the label ADHD itself and the issue of medication leave mothers in the middle feeling guilty whatever decision they make.

Four mothers in this study had boys diagnosed with ADHD (one boy also had Down syndrome and another was later diagnosed as having Asperger syndrome). These boys were all described as live wires, extremely active, strong and demanding. Anne went to her family doctor because of her son Noel's hyperactivity. At that stage she had gone through many different childminders who found Noel's behaviour unmanageable. Her doctor referred her to a child and family clinic, which Anne and her husband attended for nine months, participating in parenting and behaviour management courses hoping to solve the problems.

> So eventually I just said no, I'm not doing any more, I said we've done everything you've asked us to do and it's no different, so through that...they said 'Well, we feel that Noel is ADHD.' And it was a relief for us to know that there was something wrong with him. (Anne, mother of Noel)

Whereas Anne was 'lucky' to live in an area (suburb of a large mid-eastern city) where she was given help and support almost immediately, both Trish and Mary (living in a northern suburb of a southern city) learned about their sons' conditions by listening to a radio programme on ADHD.

> [O]n the Monday then I was in work and it was on the radio about all these children, so I rang the radio station and I said that, you know, that child, whoever, was on the radio, sounded like my child, I said, these people were describing my child, have you any contact number? (Trish, mother of Robert)

By this stage, Trish had asked for help from professionals for her son since he was having temper tantrums as a two-year-old. He had started school at the age of four, where he was considered easy to manage. At home, however, his behaviour was getting out of control, and a child psychologist who tried to assess him told Trish that 'she would have to get a barring order against him when he was 18 if he continued like this'. Despite this warning, Trish still did not know what was wrong or what to do, until the ADHD support group advised her to take Robert for a private assessment.

> So I went to [child psychiatrist]...I think he was eight. Actually, he was only seven...he had ADD...ADHD. Oppositional Defiance Disorder as well... I knew he had it, once I heard about it I knew it was him. I never had a name of what he had. I knew he had behavioural problems, but I never knew...and I never knew there was medication to help it, sure... It was a relief, yeah. Nobody wants their child to have anything, but... (Trish, mother of Robert)

Mary's general practitioner had referred her son Patrick to be assessed by a child psychologist. This psychologist dismissed Mary's worries, describing

Patrick as just immature. She recommended that Mary tried play-school for a little while to see how he got on. But Mary felt that this sort of help was not going to get her anywhere, and was relieved when she heard the radio programme.

> [H]e was so hyper...he was getting lost in the supermarket...a pure ball of energy and I felt so wrecked at one stage I did go to the doctor and said 'if you don't get this child help or take me somewhere where I can take him or do something with him, I feel like if I...put my hands on him, I will not take my hands off him', like I felt I will just kill this child if I don't get something done with him, you know. I still didn't know what Patrick had...wondering was it you as parents...was it your fault, you know, what are you doing wrong...and I was listening to the radio and they were talking about ADHD, the girls from the support group were on...and I sat there for the morning and I listened to what they were saying and it was like if they were talking about my child...and I went into town and I bought this book and I read it from cover to cover, and I said, this is what my child has, you know, and in one sense I was happy because I said, look, I said he has something and I know what it is. (Mary, mother of Patrick)

Thus not knowing was worse for these mothers than having a diagnosis such as ADHD. Not knowing means blaming yourself for your child's behaviour, and being unable to educate yourself as to what kind of help is out there. This experience was also true for Margaret, mother of Jonathan, born with Down syndrome and later displaying the same traits of extreme hyperactivity as Noel, Patrick and Robert.

> I suppose when he was younger and we would take him to Down syndrome functions there wasn't another child there who behaved like Jonathan...so I obviously expected him to be very similar to the rest of them. He's actually very, very different...so I knew there was more to it...kids that were his own age, they still were not as active, they weren't as boisterous, as loud, as destructive as him. (Margaret, mother of Jonathan)

Margaret's sense of an even greater isolation was underlined by the fact that her son did not fit in neatly into either categories of disability: he has Down syndrome but differs from the majority of children with the same condition. He has ADHD (he was eventually diagnosed privately by a paediatrician) but Margaret had never attended any of those support group meetings as she felt that nobody would really understand. 'None of those children are going to have Down syndrome. None of them...so I don't think these people will know what I'm talking about, they'll have no understanding.' Margaret's experience is a useful example of how generalizations and prejudices concerning children's disabilities can cause unnecessary suffering. Every child with Down syndrome is different and the 'placid' stereotype, as already mentioned, is more the exception than the rule.

Paradoxically, having a child who is not given a specific label from an early age can also mean that the child loses out on important early intervention. Laura's son, Kevin, for example, was described as having a language delay and a language disorder from the age of three and a half. The psychologist who assessed him initially told Laura that she would put 'query autism' on his report to the school, but only so that Kevin would be entitled to a classroom assistant when he started mainstream school. Although the psychologist kept insisting that Kevin was not autistic, Laura and her husband searched the Internet on language delays. This research, and hearing about other children with autism, made them realise that Kevin was also autistic and should have been provided with autism specific services from an early age.

> We didn't dispute when she [psychologist] said 'I think he has autism', we knew at that stage...the diagnosis was no better, they still didn't do anything for him... I mean I met her [psychologist] in the schoolyard and she said to me 'by the way, I'll be sending you out the report. He has autism and I won't be seeing him again' and she walked away...so, then it was like, wow, what does that mean, like? What difference does it make to his education? Nothing. So it has made no difference having that, you know. (Laura, mother of Kevin)

Two mothers of children initially diagnosed as severely autistic by professionals can today prove the experts wrong. Through painstaking efforts and enormous patience these mothers undertook the task to educate their children themselves at home with great success, despite the dark prognosis they had been given.

> I was very cross that he [paediatrician] could after about 40 minutes say to myself and my husband 'yeah, we're not talking hearing here...I think we're talking autism', albeit I didn't know what autism was fully, but to throw anything out in the wind, I thought, how dare you, you don't even know the child. But he said it in such a nice way, he was a lovely

> doctor…and then he said 'look, it's an area that I have no experience in whatsoever', and then I warmed to him. (Julie, mother of John)

Julie's paediatrician referred her to a speech therapist who spent an hour with Julie and four-year-old John in the room. The speech therapist consequently labelled John 'extremely autistic' and told Julie 'I very much doubt that there'll be speech.'

> I'll never forget that day… she said 'I don't even need to see him anymore.' And I said 'no follow up, no nothing?' and she said 'No, I'll report back to [paediatrician] but I wanted you to know my findings and they're serious, and there she left me… that was it, there was nothing else…and I never forget this journey back here. Never forget it. I couldn't see the road. (Julie, mother of John)

Although Brenda admitted that 'the flags went up' when her first daughter Susan stopped talking and started headbanging, she still reacted with fury over the way she was given a diagnosis of a moderate to severe degree of autism.

> I can't even remember now how exactly she put it, but the whole time she was telling me this…with absolutely no compassion, you know, she's sitting there telling me my child is doomed to a horrible life, with a grin on her face…she doesn't know the heartache that she was bringing to my table, telling me about my daughter and absolute lack of compassion. (Brenda, mother of Susan and Sally)

Brenda was living in the US when her daughter Susan was diagnosed autistic as a two-year-old. A year later, a psychological evaluation of her second daughter Sally, also resulted in the same diagnosis, moderate to severe autism. Many years later Brenda asked for the psychological tests to be redone, as she now felt that they had developed into girls with high-functioning autism, or Asperger syndrome.

> She [psychologist] said 'I'm positive that we're looking at Asperger's.' She said 'these children are not severe…they're not even moderate…I'm positive it's Asperger's'. And I said, that's all I wanted to hear. (Brenda, mother of Susan and Sally)

Intelligent but socially excluded: children with Asperger syndrome

Contemporary with Kanner was Dr Hans Asperger, a paediatrician in Vienna, who in 1944 identified a consistent pattern of abilities and behaviour in a certain group of children similar to that of Dr Kanner. His group, however, included children with average intelligence and structural language abilities. The pattern included a lack of empathy, little ability to form friendships, one-sided interests and conversation. He also found that it predominantly occurred in boys (Attwood 1998). Asperger's pioneering work did not achieve any international recognition until Lorna Wing published a paper in 1981 using the term Asperger syndrome. It is now considered a subgroup within the autistic spectrum and has its own diagnostic criteria. There is also evidence to suggest it is far more common than classic (Kanner-) autism and may be diagnosed in children who have never previously been considered autistic (Attwood 1998).

Five mothers in this study had children who were given the diagnosis of Asperger syndrome while in the school system. Four of the boys presented with much the same characteristics: poor communication and social skills. They were all of normal or above intelligence and had good academic skills. To other people they appear perfectly non-disabled and many of these children slip through the net. Those in close contact with them, however, such as mothers and teachers, will notice that they do not really fit in. Martina's son, Daniel, for example, had language difficulties and no idea of social rules such as turn-taking. His mainstream teacher suggested an assessment, where he tested above average at an IQ performance level. A speech therapist later suggested that Daniel was on the autistic spectrum, or had Asperger syndrome.

> Both my husband and myself were there and it was an initial shock and we were very upset. It took a long time to get over the initial shock. But then it was a relief. We could start to understand him and talk to him so that he could understand us. We decided to get all the information on Asperger syndrome that we could. Through the Internet and through books, we did all of that together. (Martina, mother of Daniel)

Another boy, John, a bright blue-eyed child who never stopped talking, went through his first three years at school without anyone, including his mother, Therese, noticing anything different in his behaviour. However, his teacher approached Therese one day saying that she thought he could be autistic, as he always walked away from the other children.

> I was kind of shocked...my sister then rang me one day...she was so excited over this information she found on the Internet on Asperger syndrome, and everything she read out to me described John...so I just looked up the phonebook and I found Asperger syndrome [support group], rang this person who told me what to do... So I got the book and I read the book and I was literally shaking reading the book, saying 'Oh, God, that's John, that's John', everything that was in it was John. (Therese, mother of John)

Therese took John to a child psychiatrist who confirmed the diagnosis of Asperger syndrome: 'He asked a few questions and he knew by the way he was talking to him, and he says, yes, definitely he's Asperger syndrome, can I have £100 please [laugh]'. With the diagnosis on paper Therese brought information back to the school in order to improve the situation.

> I'm glad I've discovered that there is something there so I can help him because if we didn't discover, he'd be in bits now, he'd hate going to school, he wouldn't be getting the help, he'd be way behind in his writing. (Therese, mother of John)

Marie, mother of Kevin, had always worried in the back of her mind that her son's relationship to others was not normal, and after reading about Asperger syndrome in a magazine, she contacted Aspire (Association for Asperger syndrome in Ireland) in Dublin, who recommended a child psychiatrist.

> He was diagnosed then in Junior Infants formally...at this stage I knew his diagnosis. I knew 100 per cent that this is what he had...so I brought him there and he agreed with me straight away, there was no questioning of it, that it was definitely Asperger's. (Marie, mother of Kevin)

Marie's reaction was mixed, enormously relieved to have a name for it and at the same time devastated to have it put into words. She felt she was given the diagnosis, and that was it. She did not get any help afterwards at all and she suffered from a period of depression.

> You accept it then, I suppose, you have accepted then that this...this is him now. The diagnosis was a great relief to us in that we then didn't try to push him anymore, to do stuff, stuff that we knew he'd never be able to do. (Marie, mother of Kevin)

Anne, whose son Noel had been diagnosed ADHD, was referred to a child psychiatrist by a Child and Family Clinic, when the team there suspected that Noel might also have Asperger syndrome due to his lack of social skills. This again shows that children with special needs do not fit into categories of labels easily, and that every child presents differently. Anne, having met other parents with children with ADHD, felt that Noel was again different within this group of children and welcomed the news that he also was a child on the autistic spectrum.

> We were kind of relieved then to know, because we were thinking like that his ADHD, we know children with ADHD and they don't seem to be getting into as much trouble in school as Noel was. (Anne, mother of Noel)

Mary, whose son Donal was adopted from an eastern European country, experienced huge difficulties in getting a diagnosis for her son, as much of his early problems were ascribed to his past. She recalled professionals saying: 'Well, he was adopted...what do you expect? Give him a chance.' However, when he started play-school at the age of four, his teacher raised the issue about Donal not interacting with children properly, and three years later he was also in need of speech therapy.

> She [speech therapist] said she thought he [Donal] might present with this condition that she had been reading about, Asperger syndrome, and would I try to get a diagnosis, or you know, check it out and I said of course...only to be told that there was nobody that can do it. (Mary, mother of Donal)

So Mary did what many others in the same situation had to do, she went privately to a child psychiatrist. Donal, then aged 11, was given a diagnosis of Asperger syndrome, ADHD and a question mark over Tourette syndrome (a tics disorder). Mary was left with a list of books and a list of sheets for behaviour, 'just everything you could imagine and said goodbye [laugh] and I was just left with it'. Mary reacted to the diagnosis being given from a book without reservation, without the child psychiatrist seeing the child 'for more than two minutes'. It took Mary six months of learning and reading about Asperger syndrome, to see where Donal fitted into it. She focused on Asperger and struck off the ADHD diagnosis straight away as she did not see him fitting into that category.

> Initially it [the diagnosis] was a shock. And I was terrified because I didn't know what it meant...but after the initial two, well maybe two months of terror, I was kind of glad it was something there and it wasn't me [laugh]. But it was like, oh, my God, I have to start a whole new way and I have to learn about this now and I just don't know where I'd get the energy from. (Mary, mother of Donal)

Margaret's experience of mothering sons with Asperger syndrome was vast as she had been caring for three boys born between 1985 and 1996 diagnosed with Autistic Spectrum Disorder (ASD). She also had a girl diagnosed with a language disorder. Her story was one of worry and stress, coping with babies with ear problems and severe diarrhoea, toddlers with serious behaviour problems and school children with lack of social skills. Back in 1985, when Asperger syndrome was hardly known, Margaret desperately needed to find out what was wrong with her baby who screamed and screamed non-stop.

> I was attending the hospital between the ears and the diarrhoea... I think he [the paediatrician] had a hunch...he mentioned things like not making eye contact, being worried about the child... I think he was heading in the right direction. (Margaret, mother of four children with ASD)

Unfortunately for Margaret, that paediatrician in particular was only involved in her son's case for a short while, and she had to wait another 13 years before anyone sat down and listened to her and the ball started rolling. By then she had three more children who also presented with similar problems.

> So yes, we got a diagnosis, in fact they [the neurologist and the neuropsychologist] said 'Look, within ten minutes we knew that the family had Asperger's...', that's what they said at the end but they brought us through the formality of all the testing...at this stage we knew it was Asperger syndrome, we were just waiting for someone to tell us. (Margaret, mother of four children with ASD)

Margaret was strongly in favour of getting a diagnosis of Asperger syndrome for children such as hers. She preferred this term to high-functioning autism, because of the stigma attached to autism:

> I argued that if you mention autism everyone is going to run a mile, but with Asperger's, what's that? And you can minimize it where it's necessary to minimize it... the consultant asked why we need a label, and I said

> I wanted to access the education, you need that bit of paper to go into the Department of Education so you can look for services, and I just felt they really didn't understand how bad things can be here. (Margaret, mother of four children with ASD)

All mothers agreed that receiving a diagnosis of a child's disability was a difficult emotional experience. Naturally everyone wants their children to be able to grow up healthy and happy and enjoy life to the fullest without any disability whatsoever. There are, however, as this book has documented, positive ways of breaking the news so that mothers feel comforted and given a positive outlook from the beginning. In the case of mothers of children with Down syndrome, the attitude of the professionals is of enormous importance. What they say and how they say it is very significant. In the cases of Miriam and Helen, for example, the presence of the baby together with a sympathetic paediatrician helped them to cope better with a very emotionally difficult situation.

For mothers of children with special needs like autism and/or ADHD, who are diagnosed later, it is important for professionals to listen to the mother and take on board all concerns. A label, as I have shown in this chapter, is often welcomed by these mothers who intuitively have known that something is wrong and perhaps blamed themselves for the child's behaviour. With a diagnosis they can look for help, both among professionals and within support groups. They are also able to read up on the child's condition and get information on how to deal with their child. One striking finding from these narratives, however, is that most mothers are left with a sense of emptiness after the diagnosis has been given and are at loss about where to turn for information and services. Despite a diagnosis these mothers and their children face a future full of stress and worry.

Maternal stress and severe learning disability: always at a toddler stage

To live with a child with a moderate to severe learning disability means living with a very young child who mentally never leaves the toddler stage, despite physically growing up to be a man or a woman. It means always having to watch over them to prevent accidents and keep doors and windows locked. It means dealing with temper tantrums and sometimes self-injuring behaviour. It means trying to communicate with someone who has no language skill. It could mean changing nappies on a regular basis and bathing and dressing a child who eventually grows into an adult.

> There's huge levels of stress, and certainly some dark times of course, which can be certainly depressed times and when you can't see a ray of light. (Mary, mother of Patrick)

> I have a huge sense of lack of freedom, while I absolutely love Eoin and I'm glad he's here and I wouldn't change him, I have a huge feeling of, it's a bit like serving a prison sentence and you've done no crime. (Marie, mother of Eoin)

> Windows have to be locked, doors have to be locked, bedrooms have to be locked, bathroom has to be locked, but he's able to open all those, and he takes the keys out of my pocket and opens the bedroom, opens the door, and he's gone, you know, he's way ahead of you. (Caitriona, mother of Donnacha)

Caitriona had fought long and hard, a fight culminating in the High Court, to have respite in order to survive and her son Donnacha had six nights respite every second week. He would be away from home from Wednesday night to the following Monday, 'I would be dead if I didn't [have respite] no doubts, from exhaustion.'

Mary and Marie were also constantly fighting for better services, but unfortunately their service provider was only providing them with two nights approximately every tenth week. Both these mothers had other children in the family, and were thus under enormous pressure trying to care for the child with special needs as well as his siblings. The lack of services such as respite and counselling was contributing to their high levels of stress and depression, and they were convinced that their lives could be easier if they were given more support.

> That maddens me that you have to go through this and have to feel like this when something can actually be done to avoid it, you know, to give you that little helping hand for that pull up. And it can be and it should be done. And it's just not being done. That's very maddening… When the diagnosis is made, the second step should be counselling and a list of groups and organizations and people that you can contact. A little directory should be given…and counsellors should be provided to help the feeling of being alone and coping and just to come to terms with it. (Mary, mother of Patrick)

> If prisoners get counselling, surely a mother with a child who's done nothing wrong in her life, but who is given a certain amount of...a huge prison sentence, in fact a life prison sentence, should be given counselling. That's the very least. (Marie, mother of Eoin)

Marie felt she was in need of one-to-one counselling after the diagnosis was given to her and she benefited greatly from two sessions with a psychologist. This service, however, was withdrawn very soon and Marie was left to cope on her own. She joined a parents' counselling group but felt that she did not benefit from participating in a larger group. Mary, on the other hand, joined a similar group setting where a counsellor facilitated therapy sessions for parents of children with special needs, and she found great support in that.

> It's a safe environment to leave your feelings, frustrations, you name it, out...you can talk about going through difficult patches and you can cry, you can laugh, you can use bad language, you can do whatever you like. (Mary, mother of Patrick)

Mary felt strongly that counselling should be the second step after a child has been diagnosed with a disability, together with a list of organizations and people that you can contact: 'Counsellors should be provided to help the feeling of being alone and coping and just coming to terms with it, there's so much tied up with it.' This need for counselling in order to help the mother (and the father) to cope was repeated in many of the interviews. Betty, mother of Michael, born with Down syndrome, described the experience of bringing up a child with special needs 'a hard, hard way to go' and she sees a great need for counselling:

> We didn't attend any counselling...and I often regretted I didn't...one of the things that I would love to think that we'd have in the [Down syndrome] Association...would be a counsellor there. Even attached to the hospital, that you could go to or attend afterwards, or to talk to. (Betty, mother of Michael)

Caitriona, mother of Donnacha, who is autistic, has prioritized counselling for parents in her organization: 'there should be counselling, and not just a regular psychologist, but somebody who knows what autism can cause in the family, you know, the whole family suffers because of it'.

Mothers' different ways of coping

The mothers had various ways of coping with living with a child with special needs. For example, the support from other parents and stress management had been of great importance for Mary, mother of Patrick diagnosed with ADHD. Mary described her life as being completely taken over by Patrick's condition and she went through a very bad patch 'where I felt I would kill him stone dead'. Mary was on Prozac for a while to help her cope, but she felt that attending the stress management course gave her more satisfaction:

> I found them [group sessions] good, because you were in a smaller setting, you were talking about your feelings...you weren't condemned, you weren't criticized, you were able to say things that, if you said in another place, they'd say 'Christ, what kind of mother is she like', you know...my views at times like, 'I wish the f*** I'd never had him', you know. Whereas I couldn't go up like and say that in any other, you know, and even though like, behind it all, you wouldn't mean it, but the guilt you feel while even thinking this. (Mary, mother of Patrick)

On the other hand, Anne, mother of Noel, diagnosed ADHD/Asperger syndrome, was on medication to help her cope. Noel's behaviour problem is a constant stress factor in her life: 'I've constantly been on some form of anti-depressant to help me [stay] calm with Noel.' She gave the example of his First Holy Communion as an event causing her extra worries and stress.

> It was very stressful because leading up to it I was really stressed out with it because I was wondering what way the day was going to go, he said he didn't want to take the communion and he was going to spit it out and all sorts of things. (Anne, mother of Noel)

After all her worries Noel dressed up (he wore a suit with a T-shirt underneath) and they had 'a brilliant day'. Due to his unpredictable behaviour, however, Anne had no guarantees that he would behave this particular day.

Margaret's experience of having four children with ASD had left her very vulnerable to stress and depression. Although she had learnt how to cope without the support of counselling and medication, there was a time when she was on the verge of falling apart and a family doctor prescribed anti-depressants.

> My mother had died... I ended up looking after my father... I was just torn going all places, in the caring role in every direction, and yeah, I was falling apart so I ended up on Seroxat for six months...and then we had

> John screaming and we had Charles screaming and I don't know how we came through it. (Margaret, mother of four children with ASD)

Margaret's situation is an example of how a mother can learn to cope with existing conditions, but how new added stressors such as other illnesses in the family can change the situation dramatically. Margaret had experienced the early years with her first child as extremely difficult. He screamed and screamed non-stop and she felt very isolated at home in the housing estate all day while her husband was at work. She believed that breastfeeding her baby saved his life.

> I think I breastfed him for just over a year, and I think when he was an infant I would have strangled him if I hadn't breastfed him, cause I used to put him to the breast when I felt really anxious. Then when he weaned, he weaned himself, I used to put him in the cot, when I felt that he was under threat... I just dumped him in the cot and ran out, I ran downstairs so at least he was safe. (Margaret, mother of four children with ASD)

Screaming and temper tantrums are obviously huge stress factors for all mothers, and for those who mother children with special needs this type of behaviour occurred frequently. However, there are children who are generally placid but who can also inflict another type of stress on the mother. This is particularly true for those children who withdraw from social activities and friends or whose potential learning abilities are not met due to specific difficulties such as using language appropriately.

> Even since he learnt to speak, he's been speaking in a context he shouldn't be...he's ahead of his years if you know what I mean, and for a child, like he would have big words...that he didn't really understand, and used them out of context and he still would be like that today... definitely it's been very stressful... I have found it very, very difficult, I was more of a sociable person before, I find it difficult now to be. That's on the negative side. (Mary, mother of Donal)

In Mary's situation the stress was mainly inflicted by the lack of understanding from professionals and the lack of services for Donal. She, like many other mothers, spent a lot of time on the phone, searching for advice and support. This constant pressure of having to make phone calls was wearing her down more so than her son's condition. Walking was her way of coping, and taking a break from the phone calls.

> I walk. I walk [laugh]. I've got so many pairs of walking shoes worn out at this stage and I walk quite a bit and I read and I lay low, and I take notes of the next ste…when I'm ready and able and when I'm not mentally tired anymore. Yeah, because that is what happens, I get really mentally drained, you know, and it, of course it affects me, but more often than not, I would say, I'm a positive person and I see the positive sides in most things I do. (Mary, mother of Donal)

Martina, mother of Daniel, who has Asperger syndrome, found the loneliness and lack of understanding from schools in particular most stressful and depressing. Daniel had no behaviour problems, but was in need of speech therapy and social skills training, services that were not provided. Martina spent hours on the phone to various governmental departments and service providers and described her life as going 'up and down'.

> What do I do to cope? I suppose I just get down, I might talk to, might ring my mother or, my mother more than anyone else, because I find that nobody else would really, nobody else understands, you know, I might talk to my husband. (Martina, mother of Daniel)

The invaluable support of the participants' mothers was a recurring theme in the interviews. A strong bond between mothers and daughters was helping many of these women cope. Brenda praised the help and support from her mother, when she was on her own with her two girls diagnosed severely autistic as very young.

> My mother. That was it. My mother has just been my saviour. She was there all the time, because with two of them, you can't go into the grocery store, you can't do anything, so I mean, just to go and get groceries, there would have to be the two of us. (Brenda, mother of Susan and Sally)

Brenda, like many of the other mothers, described the early years as the most difficult for her, with the two girls then being young and low functioning and her husband not supportive at all. She recalled in particular having to sleep on the floor outside the girls' bedroom in fear of them getting out of the house and drowning in a nearby stream that was not fenced off. This situation reflects a reality for many mothers of children with learning disability living with the fear that something would happen to their children.

To mothers with severely learning disabled children, the stress and depression of mothers with high-functioning autistic children might not appear to be such a daunting task of mothering. Their children go to mainstream school, function independently in so many ways and are not in need of constant supervision. It is, however, important to acknowledge the worries of these mothers. It might not be the same as for the mothers of the child with a severe disability, but they are nevertheless affecting their lives negatively. Marie, mother of Kevin, diagnosed with Asperger syndrome, described her emotional stress involved in trying to help him form relationships and prevent him from getting hurt and bullied.

> My life is totally wrapped up in him really... I'd be more stressed than a regular [mother] because I'm always watching, and I'm always aware of, when there's children here playing, I always have an ear out. (Marie, mother of Kevin)

While the majority of my participants felt that their children's special needs, directly or indirectly, inflicted more stress and depression than anything else in their lives, some mothers found other life experiences, such as the work environment, more stressful. This was the case for Therese, whose son John was diagnosed with Asperger syndrome. John's condition had the potential of inflicting more stress and depression on Therese, but in her opinion, it was her work situation that made her ill (see Chapter 4), never her son's special needs. Nevertheless, Therese experienced pressure trying to help John improve his handwriting in school and do his homework. His exaggerated affection could also sometimes get too much for her:

> He does take an awful lot of energy, yeah... You could be running late in the morning going to school and he insists on a hug and a kiss, putting his coat on and his arms are wrapped around me and 'Mummy, hug me, I love you', he drives me mad... I say 'John, just relax, I know you love me, you told me ten times today already', you know, but it's not his fault. (Therese, mother of John)

Therese accepted John's difference with a positive attitude, his constant interrupting when she talks to friends or watches television, his way of talking about people with no consideration of whether they would be hurt or not 'Look, that man is as fat as a pig' and his own ways of reasoning. Although 'I don't want John to have anything wrong with him' she was determined that whatever he needed, she was going to help him.

> I don't feel depressed with him being the way he is now, I'm just happy there is something there that is recognized, that'll help him... He stresses

> me with his homework and that...when he's in bed fast asleep, I say 'ah, here's the poor fellow who has a mother like me', I've probably caused him more hassle then he causes me. (Therese, mother of John)

In Therese's case a diagnosis and subsequent reading on how to deal with a child with Asperger syndrome helped her cope with her son. She had suffered from severe post-natal depression after the birth of her first child and this in combination with a difficult situation at work had made her very ill with an eating disorder. Nevertheless, she accepted her son's special needs and found that the school was very supportive 'from the teachers...the fact that there's actually a label put on him now...we can kind of relax a bit with him...we understand him'.

For many mothers helping the children has been their way of coping. Julie, mother of John, diagnosed as severely autistic as a four-year-old and now high functioning, described the helplessness of not knowing what to do as most difficult:

> [T]he only time I felt angry was when I didn't have anything that I could hold on to. Once I got the ABA [Applied Behaviour Analysis] manual and there was something that I could actually do to help this child, then I was fine. (Julie, mother of John)

Julie decided to learn everything she could about autism on the Internet. Consequently she felt empowered by this knowledge and decided to help John as much as she could herself. Friends and relatives told her she would 'go nuts' by spending all her time and energy on teaching John herself, but she convinced herself that this was necessary and that she would keep going as long as she had to.

Miriam felt the same about her son William, who has Down syndrome. Miriam described herself as an optimist with an interest in alternative medicine and yoga, and when she found out about a special programme to follow to enhance William's development, she embarked on it. Her way of coping had been to acknowledge the grief of a child who could have been, but also to focus on the child who is there.

> Having William was sort of...something new was going to happen...and having a child with special needs then throws you into meeting a whole new set of people and a whole new life that you never knew existed. (Miriam, mother of William)

Miriam's attitude to this 'new world' was positive, referring to the support and friendship she had met along the way. Having a child with special needs, however, will also bring about a whole new world of professionals – some of whom might not always be that sympathetic.

Professionals: helpful or adding to the stress?

As soon as a child is diagnosed with a learning disability, and often while parents are looking for help, professionals such as social workers, speech therapists, psychologists, psychiatrists and so on become part of their lives. In many cases, opening the door to professionals means a loss of privacy and can also cause a lot of stress:

> I think fairly soon after we came home, within certainly a few weeks...the social worker from the service provider got in touch with us and then she came out to visit. And we had both to be there for her to visit, which had to be something like three o'clock in the afternoon, which meant that [husband] had to come home from work... If you never had social workers visiting before it was kind of 'oh, what is it going to be like?'...and it was very low key, you know, no information really, or nothing that we hadn't read in the parent pack. (Miriam, mother of William)

> Before we saw the first psychologist, a social worker came first...he was useless, I'd say he's long retired now, he...I'd say he knew nothing about autism... he just told me he had to come before the psychologist could come, I never really knew why he was here, didn't want to see me again, there was nothing... he came to the door, which I was really annoyed [with] because I had a good few friends in here having coffee and he came to the door and said really loudly 'I'm a social worker and I've come to talk to you about Kevin'... I mean luckily they were close friends so it was ok, but I just thought, you know... He was very nice when he sat down, but I just thought he was useless. (Laura, mother of Kevin)

The quotes above confirm that there was an obvious stigma around a visit from a social worker and perhaps a fear of being scrutinized and observed by a stranger. Contributing to a sense of discomfort in these two cases was the lack of control the mothers had over the time of the social worker's visit: 'it had to be...three o'clock' and 'he came to the door'. I would argue that not facilitating the families and, even worse, turning up without making a phone call, showed disrespect for parents and did not consider their needs and views.

One of my participants had taken a strong stand against the 'invasion' of her private life and home:

> [M]aybe I was just odd, very odd, but I never want my home contaminated by any of them [professionals] that's the way I looked at it, if there was a speech therapist, or an occupational therapist, or a psychologist for that matter that belonged down the clinic or the school...it did not belong in our home, and I'm still the same today, that I'm very, very finicky about who will sit here...because I do believe that they...in that clinical side of it contaminates the lovely home you have. (Julie, mother of John)

One mother recalled an event where she saw a risk of the social worker jumping to conclusions about her 'abusing' her son:

> [I]n the end of the day he's a social worker so he has to be aware of whether this child is in a home where he's being battered [laugh] you know, and it was actually afterwards when I was telling [husband]... [husband] was kind of, you know, 'oh, my God' like you know 'if we hit him are we going to be' you know 'on charges'. (Anne, mother of Noel)

Anne had told the social worker about an incident when her son had driven her to smash a pizza in his face: Noel had requested the pizza but shoved it off the table when a corner was cut off it and he continued to scream and kick until Anne lost her temper. To a social worker and any professional working with children, this incident is very serious. To a mother living with a child with autism or ADHD this incident is understandable and is probably not uncommon, although most mothers would keep this to themselves. Anne was honest and brave to talk about what had happened and also described her feeling of guilt afterwards:

> And of course then, when that happens I run in here and I'm roaring and crying and I feel so guilty over what I'm after doing... I lifted him up and I hugged him and told him I was sorry and he kept saying 'But Mummy, you smashed that pizza into my face and it hurt' and I said 'But Noel, you asked me for that pizza and then you tell me you won't eat it because I took a tiny piece of it'... So I said 'Will you eat it now?' and he said 'yeah', so we heated it up for him and he sat down and ate the pizza. (Anne, mother of Noel)

This is an example of a mother who is pushed to her limits and needs all the help she can get in order to cope with her child. But instead of providing her with practical support, such as frequent respite or home help, a social worker comes to her house to take notes of incidents and challenges her confidence as a mother. All she is left with is a guilty conscience and a worried husband.

Another example of a mother's frustration over professionals' negative interference is Helen, mother of Andrew, born with Down syndrome. She had struggled for years to have her son accepted into a mainstream school:

> When my husband and I went to speak to her [the principal] concerning Andrew going into the school, we told her that he had Down syndrome. She said 'Down syndrome, snotty nose and frothing of the mouth'... those were her very words... There was no question of a little boy, that was her conclusion, that was what she knew about Down syndrome. I was scandalized! I couldn't believe a professional would come out with a statement like that... So I mean that was a good indicator of that we had ahead of us really. (Helen, mother of Andrew)

Andrew was eventually accepted into mainstream and Helen continued to look for support. However, the team of teacher, resource teacher, social worker and psychologist only reacted swiftly when they heard that she smacked her child:

> [T]he review case ended and the next week I got a call in from the psychologist about smacking Andrew. 'Did I not know that it was against health board's regulations [in the context of pre-school staff] to smack my child?... How do you smack him? Where do you smack him? What part of his body do you smack? How often do you do it? When do you do it? With what do you do it?' And I said 'Hold on here for a second', there was a major problem, people do not understand the difference between smacking your child, which is correction, and beating your child, which is a completely different ballgame'. So I said to the psychologist 'Are you telling me now that my name is on a list somewhere because I smack my child?... Two review meetings for Andrew within a fortnight of each other? I said 'It usually takes a year and it's very hard to get.' I said 'I'm not an idiot.' (Helen, mother of Andrew)

Regardless of the regulations concerning 'smacking' children in Ireland, many parents still do. More than half of 500 parents reported that they smack their children, according to a recent survey (Ring 2003). I do not attempt to go into the debate of whether it is right or not to smack children. What I want to show with the quote above is that a mother of a non-disabled child would not be scrutinized over smacking a child, because she would hardly be involved with a professional team of teachers, social workers and psychologists. Paradoxically, a mother who is beaten by her child is left to deal with it herself:

> The health nurse...was looking at me as if I had ten heads. I asked her had they a system, because the school told me that there is a system where somebody would come in and do his homework with him every day and then I could go out then for that hour... She never heard of it, she said... Like I've even had social workers to put him into foster care...that was years ago now. They did nothing. I rang them, I rang them about eight months ago and said that I couldn't cope with him. They said 'ah, he's not at risk', there's nothing they can do. (Trish, mother of Robert)

In Trish's case it was her son Robert who physically assaulted her in their home so badly she had to take time off work and contacted the social workers for support. But the fact that she did not hurt him in any way consequently deprived her of any help whatsoever from the authorities. This is an example of how society ignores mothers crying out for help for their children. I can fully understand the dilemma for social workers trying to determine whether a child is at risk or not. There is, however, a need for a greater professional understanding of the maternal context in cases like the two mentioned above (Helen and Trish).

There is a danger in portraying the mother-child relationship as something unconditionally positive. Featherstone (1997, 1999), a feminist writer on social work and child abuse, addresses this ambivalence in the context of children at risk of abuse. She calls for an increased engagement with the relationship between mothering and what children need. Furthermore, she urges professionals, and women social workers in particular, to be aware of their own cultural expectations of motherhood. Featherstone argues that this awareness is critical in order to listen to mothers and take them seriously, and provide help where it is really needed. This awareness is even more important in the context of mothering a child with special needs. I would argue that many mothers, who do their utmost out of love and affection for their child with special needs, have their efforts minimized and criticized by people who are supposed to be helpful. As mentioned earlier, social workers and public health nurses were often criticized by the mothers for making life more difficult:

> I had fierce problems actually getting a copy of that first psychological assessment, the social worker from the service provider called and she

> was saying 'We'll send a copy to your GP and he'll discuss the relevant paragraphs or whatever with you.' I said to her 'Jonathan is my own child and you're telling me I can't have the information about him... I am entitled to read it.' And she said 'Parents don't always understand these things' and I said, 'Well, that's fine...I'm actually quite used to reading them, but if I don't understand I'll ask.' So I did get it, but it really was against their better judgement that I got it... I feel that they're talking down to me, yeah. Some of them, not all of them... I sometimes think they think I'm hysterical, 'that's just another mother'... Some of them are fine now, some of them will listen. (Margaret, mother of Jonathan)

Another mother, Julie, expressed her frustration over the lack of understanding from professionals as she went to collect free nappies for her son:

> So I thought, Good Lord above, a woman asking for a five-year-old to have nappies, isn't that bad enough, like will you just give me a pack of nappies and I'll come back when I need another one, but it took me awhile to get used to that, to go down to that clinic and to sign out those nappies, you're made to feel very, you know...that I'm coming here robbing something from the state. (Julie, mother of John)

Similarly, child psychiatrists and paediatricians sometimes made the mothers feel inferior and scrutinized:

> I just asked him directly at the time [child psychiatrist] are we talking autism or? And I remember that he said, he was so evasive and rude, and you know, 'Oh, you're a very direct person', and I was actually totally thrown, the reason he was there was actually to see how you and your husband were getting on, like it was, how dare they think they're entitled to see how your marriage... We had no problem with our marriage, it was our child. (Marie, mother of Eoin)

> and she was saying 'Oh, Dr Whatever It Is, is a very good doctor' and I said 'maybe she is, but she certainly doesn't have the personality to deal with me, you know, to make me feel at ease or whether I have a hope of getting this [Domiciliary Care Allowance] I felt immediately they were saying 'You're looking for money off us, you know, and I mean, as people said to me, it's not something you're getting every week, it's once a month you're getting this, this payment, you know.' (Anne, mother of Noel)

> I felt that I was treated coldly by the paediatrician because I've gone back to him since and it's kind of him looking over his glasses, like 'who are you telling me', you know...and I've got the freedom of information chart in which he says 'I think Mrs Murphy is grasping at straws', you know, that was actually his words, so whether he thought I wasn't clever enough. (Caitriona, mother of Donnacha)

Another place where mothers felt unsupported and criticized was in the schools:

> They [mainstream school] were angry and said they felt betrayed because I hadn't told them [about Daniel having Asperger syndrome] beforehand. And they said 'He's weird, he's odd and strange.' I left crying and I haven't been near the principal. I also rang the Department of Education and asked them where could he go if this school didn't keep him? I told them that he has a right to an education. (Martina, mother of Daniel)

> I remember going down for a parent–teacher meeting and this would have been obviously his first year. And as soon as I walked in she just says 'Well, what can I say' and...she wasn't going on about how he was progressing, you know, in his academics...it was all about, you know, how disruptive he was and all that, and I sat through the whole thing sobbing my heart out. I really, you know, this is my child she's talking about... She was saying kind of 'We know he's ADHD but like he's just disruptive in the class, he won't sit down, he's always making noises trying to get all the other kids in trouble' and things like that, you know, so we had no answer for her. (Anne, mother of Noel)

Both Martina and Anne were reduced to tears after being told about their sons' behaviour. It was not as if they were unaware of this already, they had looked for help for years and were still fighting for support. The fact that many schools lack resources to meet the needs of children with special needs cannot be denied but I would question why the pressure was put back onto the parents instead of the schools joining them in their struggle for proper help.

Although the mothers' experiences of dealing with professionals were mainly negative, there were a few good exceptions. Speech therapists, for example, were given a lot of credit by some of the participants:

> [T]he speech therapist, I think she was probably the person who has been the most helpful through the years really, and she helped them [children

> in the special school] as much as she could and she got information. (Mary, mother of Donal)

Another mother felt that the social worker was a great support to both herself and her husband:

> Our social worker, now I must admit, for a couple of years, would have been certainly a great support to [husband]...we haven't had a social worker since March, they haven't replaced that social worker that left...that's a huge void as well. We both miss that terribly. (Mary, mother of Patrick)

> I'm very, very lucky with this principal too, as well in this school. And from day one, the teacher that he had, he had her for two years, even though, like the minute he went in, he clicked with her straight away. And they got on very, very well... The class was smaller. You couldn't pay for this education...there's no problem in talking to the principal, he always has time for you, he'll always talk to you, you know, there's no problem at all in getting the principal, to talk to him. (Mary, mother of Patrick)

> Anyway, when he was diagnosed with the Asperger's, the school decided to apply for a resource teacher...and she is brilliant with him and he absolutely loves going to her... There was one day when the headmaster rang [husband] and of course, [husband thought] 'oh, God, what's wrong' and the headmaster says, 'I'm ringing you to tell you' he says 'that he's behaving quite well', and he says 'I thought I'd ring you with a more positive phone call than all the negative ones you get.' (Anne, mother of Noel)

The quotes above indicate that some professionals understand the needs of parents to hear a positive word about their child's behaviour. This support, such as a positive phone call from a principal, is greatly appreciated by mothers who, often, are at the receiving end of 'bad' news. Some mothers also praised whole support systems available through certain service providers:

> Very soon after Andrew was born we would have gone on a course, run by [service provider], for parents with children with Down syndrome and that was wonderful... It went on for maybe four–six weeks and both partners were encouraged to go to it...just to discuss different things, and they gave us information and they would...talk us through things, services that were available and support systems and all the rest of it.

> Now, I could not speak highly enough of [service provider], they were wonderful. (Helen, mother of Andrew)

Proper support systems where the whole family is looked after and where the child's needs are being met were something that Margaret wished that all families could be provided with:

> Support structures for the family...and it's not always necessarily special needs...if there is problems, send somebody into the home to take the pressure off, because the difference between coping and not coping is being able to work through your problem, or collapsing, to such an extent that the children will end up, it's the children will end up in court, or on the streets or whatever. Early intervention, support the family, provide parenting counselling, provide parenting classes, I have to say I've benefited from those, just ordinary ones in the school, support the family through the stages... All the services that the child needs should be accessed through the schooling, through the normal school, without having to travel. (Margaret, mother of four children)

Examples of existing good services could encourage less fortunate mothers to fight harder to change their own situations. Running through the narratives was a sense of resilience against poor quality services and unsupportive professionals. This maternal resistance has also been documented by other researchers on mothers of children with disabilities (Malacrida 2003; Read 2000). Similarly the majority of the mothers in my study seemed determined not to let the professionals stand in their way when it came to improving the situation for their children:

> So I'm very much of the mind that when Patrick does get care, and I'm going to fight tooth and nail for this, we [husband and her] both are, that it'll be the care that we want him to get... There are no small gods, for want of a better word, anymore. People don't take what's handed and given to them anymore. You'd be surprised, there are still an amount of people who do unfortunately, but this day of getting what you're given and be grateful for it is long gone and buried. (Mary, mother of Patrick)

One year after our initial meeting, Mary had gone to a solicitor and with the help of his support had increased the respite for her son Patrick to every second weekend. This gave her and the rest of her family a chance to have some normal life together, which was very important to her. Other mothers also spoke about the 'God-complex' and how they had been brought up as 'good Irish girls' but the experience of having a child with special needs had changed their attitudes:

> You're not looking for God to come down [off] his cross, like, and to be given...you know, you're just looking for something, you know, a little bit, because you're stuck with this life seven days a week, 365 days a year, you're stuck with this. (Mary, mother of Patrick)

> I have no fear at all [laugh]...I wouldn't care now, I just wouldn't care, and if I had something on my mind now, wouldn't care if it was a crowded room, I would say it...cause I felt we had to go through so much and there was so little help out there for us, and now I just wouldn't care. (Betty, mother of Michael)

> I wouldn't lie down as easy. You know, I got stronger from them [professionals]. (Julie, mother of John)

> They [mainstream school] gave us a hard time about it, but in the end of the day I said 'Even if you said you weren't [taking him] he's coming here. We're in the catchment's area...he's [principal] been great ever since, he's realized that I fight if I have to [laugh]. (Laura, mother of Kevin)

> [T]he way I was brought up, you did as you were told, and these people know what they're talking about, well, in actual fact I've learned that a lot of people don't know what they're talking about, do you know what I mean? I know a lot more than they do. (Therese, mother of John)

> They [professionals] seemed to be intimidated by people knowing too much, or knowing too little, or knowing what they thought was too much... In fact, I think they get intimidated very easily, which I found actually funny, you know, that they have all this knowledge and would be intimidated by a mother just asking some sensible questions... I think there's a God complex out there. (Marie, mother of Eoin)

> I was trying to be the Good Irish Girl who's quiet...but I think this is probably my personality has been brought out, the real me. So something good has come out of it... I probably feel that I didn't realize I had all this ability until this happened... I had to fight, for everything I ever got for Donnacha, I had to fight for it. (Caitriona, mother of Donnacha)

The voices above indicated a change in the ways the mothers saw themselves in relation to professionals and service providers. Referring to the past and looking to the future, they were prepared to fight for their children's rights to a greater extent than before. They were not letting themselves be patronized by anybody and they had enough knowledge to feel confident about themselves. They wanted to be taken seriously by any professional who came into their lives to provide service and support for their child with a learning disability. Most of all, they wanted to be listened to and treated as equals, in a partnership.

> I'd like them [professionals] first of all to treat me as an equal, because I used to feel that the psychologist was really analysing me rather than the child... And I think an awful lot of parents agree with me there and...if they would treat us, especially nowadays parents are so well up with Internet and with everything, we're not stupid. (Caitriona, mother of Donnacha)

> For those who are applying the diagnostic services, please do not minimize parents, listen to what they're saying, if you don't agree, if you feel, yeah, things are over the top, say nothing, but don't put parents down because they'll stop talking. Don't blame the parents for their child's behaviour. Children, or maybe if it is...because of marriage break up, it still shouldn't minimize the reason, they still need help. That's the first thing. (Margaret, mother of four children with ASD)

> Listen to Mum! Not only for special needs, every mother. This crack that they spout off 'Mum knows best', they don't, they say that when they don't even, it's only lip service, but if only they believed in it, because it is very, very true. Mothers are given a very special gift, even more than fathers, mothers are given a sense of knowing when their child is very upset about something. We have it in us. I really believe that. We feel their feelings and for professionals not to listen to that, and to dismiss, and they do it all the time. (Julie, mother of John)

> And I think there is, I mean there must be an intuitive thing there with mothers, that they might not even know the reasons for something, but they just know something should be done, or they know something...we all got numerous stories we could tell and in the end, two years later, mother was proved right, you know, this kind of thing. But I suppose, you see, when there's no scientific proof there, I mean, how could you verify that, which you can't, but you're actually not listened to. (Miriam, mother of William)

These mothers felt strongly that maternal thinking is of great importance when discussing a child with a learning disability and deciding what support services are needed. The general consensus was that many professionals seemed to minimize or ignore that thinking. In the past, lack of information and education made these mothers vulnerable and more inclined to accept professional advice. This is changing as the Internet is opening up the 'scientific' world also to mothers and will have long lasting effects on the relationship between parents and professionals.

Conclusion

When a child is diagnosed with a disability such as Down syndrome, autism or ADHD, the mother's initial reaction is naturally one of grief. My participants confirmed this feeling of shock and sadness, but they all found ways to overcome this grief and adjust their lives accordingly. A poem entitled *Welcome to Holland* (Kingsley 1987) is frequently passed around and read by parents of newly diagnosed children. In this poem the metaphor of planning a holiday abroad is used to describe the experience of having a child with special needs. The expectant parents (usually the mother) read guidebooks and learn the language of the place they are planning to visit, in this case Italy. They are well prepared for this trip when they finally embark on it: when the child is born. However, instead of landing in Italy (having a non-disabled child that fits into society) the plane takes them to Holland (the manuals on childcare prove to be useless). It takes them a while to adjust, but soon they discover the joys of Holland. They buy new guidebooks, learn a new language and despite losing the dream of Italy (grieving the loss of a non-disabled child), they feel free to enjoy the very lovely things about Holland (the child that is there).

There are certainly positive things about having a child who is different and the mothers in this book never denied their love for their children. I would, however, argue that the difficulties in getting appropriate help and support (buying new guidebooks and learning a new language) make it very hard for mothers to cope. Mothers of children born with Down syndrome, for example, learn almost immediately that they have 'landed in Holland' as their children are diagnosed shortly after birth. The 'tour guides', however, vary in the way they deal with the mothers. It is therefore vital that professionals such as paediatricians, nurses or social workers make the mother feel welcome in this 'new country' by being sympathetic and positive. Similarly, classical autism and severe learning disabilities are usually diagnosed during the child's first years, although 'the arrival to Holland' is delayed for some time and leaves the mother in a limbo not knowing where she is going. This uncertainty is even more evident for mothers of children with high-functioning autism/Asperger syndrome and ADHD. The mother often knows for years that things are not the way they should be – she was sitting on the plane destined for Italy, but is now circling aimlessly around in the sky. Many of my participants described the diagnosis as a welcome relief as they at long last have an explanation to their child's abnormal behaviour. Using the metaphor of the journey again, they finally land in a country with some form of guidance available. Exactly how they get on in this new country, however, strongly depends upon what supports are available.

Living with a child with special needs is not easy and the narratives of my 18 participants were all full of sadness and hopelessness. They were exhausted, stressed and often depressed. Despite the variation between the different disabilities (from Down syndrome to Asperger syndrome, from severe learning disability to high intelligence, from severe behaviour problems to placidity), these mothers of children with special needs had to struggle extra hard in order to get on with life. They chose many different ways of coping with this stress and depression. Some of the mothers found counselling beneficial and those who had not been provided with any form of counselling expressed a need for it (Sanders and Morgan 1997). The support given by close relatives or other mothers in similar situations was often seen as positive (Ainbinder *et al.* 1998; Dumas *et al.* 1991; Lovenfosse and Viney 1999). The ability to do something to enhance the child's development was also seen as an important coping factor for some mothers who were faced with poor services or no services at all.

Many of the mothers expressed a refusal to accept the current situation of little or no services available. They demanded that they, as mothers of children with learning disabilities, should be treated as equals and listened to by professionals in order to meet their children's needs better. As mothers they felt that they had both knowledge and skills in dealing with their children and that professionals should be aware of this 'maternal' knowledge. If mothers were given a chance to plan and design services for children with special needs, the incidents of stress and struggle would probably be minimized. Furthermore, these women would also have more options as regards to their own personal choices of life fulfilment. This theme will be discussed in the next chapter.

Chapter 4

Maternal Work and Employment

> It seems to me that a huge amount of energy is being used by mothers to go out and find answers. How can we get to the stage where this expenditure of energy is turned into quality time for the child? Doesn't it seem so senseless?
>
> (Miriam, mother of William)

This chapter discusses the issue of the mother's employment and how a child with a learning disability impacts on her choice of occupation and personal fulfilment. The first part takes a closer look at deciding factors regarding the mother's choice of a career and employment outside the home versus staying at home full time. I will also discuss the issue of the 'maternal work' involved in mothering a child with special needs, where mothers provide training and education for their own children. Second, the chapter explores the time and energy invested by the mothers in dealing with professionals and service providers for the purpose of helping their child. Finally, I analyse mothers' vision of themselves and their children in the future.

Staying at home: a positive choice

All 18 mothers in this study had been engaged in work outside the home prior to the birth of their children and their decision to cease work was not necessarily in connection with the child with special needs. In some cases older siblings or other family circumstances had influenced their decision to stay at home full time and in this sense the gender divided roles are following the pattern of Irish families in general (McCarthy 1995). Ten of the eighteen mothers were at home full time at the time of the initial meeting. Nine of these women were married to men who were in skilled/managerial breadwinning positions and the single mother received maintenance from the children's father. It is important to remember that the majority of these mothers belonged to the middle class/upper working class. The following quotes give examples of the reasons why the mothers listed above left their jobs:

> I had planned to keep working after Patrick had arrived, but then there was the death of my husband's mother and my father, and then I ended up sort of taking on some of the home situation, because some of my husband's family were still at home. And that would have changed my working situation... I would have gone back to work sort of part time in and out between three of the children and I gave it up formally after the birth of our third child. (Mary, restaurant worker and childcarer)

> I wasn't in a position to work, because [daughter] was tiny and [husband] is not the type of person who would stay at home being a house-husband [laugh] even now when it's more acceptable. (Miriam, business-partner with husband)

> [My husband] is out and I'm at home. And that's by choice! I was so glad to give up work, I mean, I had worked for years, I was so happy to say goodbye to it. I had no desire to go back to work, I mean my husband would have said to me, would you not think now to get yourself a little job, and I'd say, no, I'm happy to be here! (Helen, office worker)

> I stopped working. I had actually stopped at about five months, it was a very unsuccessful attempt going back... I suppose I would have been a person that would have thought I would have always worked, and you know, nothing, hell or high water wouldn't have stopped me, but then when I had my first child, part of me really wanted to stay at home and be a mother, but this sort of thing of 'oh, you don't do that', but in a way Eoin allowed me the, I wouldn't say the luxury of staying at home and be a mother, because it's not a luxury either, it's a choice, allowed me the choice because I just decided no one really could care for him the way I could. I would have needed a very good excuse to give up work and that was my excuse, do you know what I mean? (Marie, self-employed therapist)

Mary, Miriam, Helen and Marie were all happy to stay at home full time and this decision had little to do with the fact that they had a child with a learning disability. Mary's firstborn was diagnosed with special needs at an early age, yet it was not until Mary's third child was born that she gave up her job completely. Miriam had given up her job after the birth of her daughter, long before the arrival of her third child who was born with Down syndrome. Helen and Marie felt happier to stay at home than to continue to work and experienced great fulfilment as full-time mothers. Other mothers were happy staying at home while the children were young but planned to return to work at a later stage:

> We both worked in the bank. Then we had to [financially]. I continued after Daniel was born, but when number two came along I stayed at home. It didn't pay to get childminders and I felt good about staying at home. I don't want to go back to work until they are in their teens. I'd like to study now, but I couldn't go back to work and leave Daniel with a childminder. He would probably be put in front of a television. (Martina, bank official)

> I would hate to leave home to go to work because he draws great comfort from the fact that I'm here waiting for him when he comes home, and, or just that I'm at the school gate, he hates having anyone else to pick him up and you know, I feel he needs that while he's young really. (Marie, teacher)

Anne, Brenda and Margaret were mothers who did give up their work because of their children with special needs:

> We felt it was too difficult for me to work full time. And we said, well, we're gonna have to think of something else here, like, see if I could get some sort of job closer to home, part time, something, and I had worked for 20 years with the same company and all and having to give it up, like I mean, it was a big thing for me to give up... Other people gave up work when they had children, I never did, I always worked, and now I'm actually enjoying the fact that I'm not working and [my husband] likes me not working. (Anne, shop manager)

> I had already sold the big house and found a small house that needed work, so that I could be free of a mortgage and I could be free of him [husband]...it gave me the freedom not to be under a mortgage and not have to be under someone's thumb because I couldn't go to work, you know, I had these children, so it was like, what are you going to do? Well, you're gonna scale down. (Brenda, interior designer)

> My grand plan, which totally changed of course with the children [laugh], was that, I loved teaching, I really loved it...and my grand plan was that I would have a family and that I would give up full-time teaching, in order to concentrate on my writing, which now I had been pretty successful at. My grand plan, which I think would have worked would the children have been normal, would have been to have childcare in the mornings, do my work, and I can't write any other time of the day, so it was just going to be ideal, writing is so intense that two–three hours a day is plenty, and that I would be a very much a full-time mother for the rest of the day, and I think, you know, had that worked, it's wonderful for both mother and child, cause you'd have had a few hours a day, but the bulk of the day would be as a full-time mother. But it didn't work. (Margaret, teacher/writer)

The quotes above indicate that all of these mothers felt that it was in the best interest of the child (or children) that they remained at home full time and the decision was thus looked upon favourably. One mother stated that she herself had no interest in going back to work after her children were born, regardless of one child's disability and that this was a choice she deliberately made (Helen). Likewise, Marie had felt under 'pressure' to keep up her work and needed a good excuse to stay at home and it was paradoxically her son's disability that 'allowed' her this choice. It is important to acknowledge that these ten mothers were in a financial position to stay at home, most importantly due to a breadwinning partner or other assets.

In one case, where the mother's income was part of the budget, the decision was more difficult:

> I decided to give up work...and we [husband and Anne] said we would see what I could do, as in where I could get money...well, we had always got my income... So like this was coming as a big drop. (Anne, mother of Noel)

In Anne's case it was her son Noel's behaviour problems that forced her to give up her job as a supervisor in a shop. She had tried to combine a career and mothering for several years, changing from full time to part time, before she finally gave it up:

> So eventually then I got a job in a shop, working at six o'clock in the morning until ten. So that way I didn't need a child minder... I was still having difficulties with Noel, which meant that at night, when I was

> trying to get to bed early, cause I was up at six, and it would be difficult to get him to bed, and then [husband] was having an awful lot of trouble in the morning trying to get him ready for school...but we stuck that out for, I stuck that out for a year and a half, and it came to the stage where I was having difficulties kind of working and keeping my mind on work, really, with Noel. I was having a lot of difficulties with it really. (Anne, mother of Noel)

The lack of childcare was the main reason why Anne could not keep working. She had gone through many childminders from the time Noel was very young, but due to his challenging behaviour they did not last long. Anne's case is an example of a situation where the only person willing and capable of caring for her son was she herself and all attempts to find alternative childcare failed. At the time of the follow-up meeting, Anne had started to mind another child for a woman working full time, and she seemed to be content doing this kind of work in her own home. This way she managed to make a financial contribution to the family income without having to rely on external childcare facilities. Similarly, research on maternal employment and children with special needs undertaken in the UK and the US (Baldwin and Carlisle 1994; Booth and Kelly 1998; Lewis, Kagan and Heaton 2000; Shearn and Todd 2000; Warfield Erickson and Hauser-Cram 1996) documents the difficulties this group of mothers have trying to find appropriate childcare.

The decision to give up a career appeared to have caused more emotional difficulties for the mother who had felt very satisfied with her work (Margaret, writer/teacher) as opposed to the mothers who did not share the same positive feelings towards their jobs.

> It's very hard to see young women writers who are doing very well in Ireland in our days, and I've missed the boat. That's hard... I've started writing again... I'm not going to get great commissions, I can't even take on a great commission, big commission because I can't commit. I don't know when I'm going to have a crisis, you know. When you get established you start looking around and you get commissioned and there's a date and a deadline set. I could not commit to that because something could happen with the kids, and I'd be so stressed out from trying to deal with it so what I'm doing, I'm just working freelance for myself. (Margaret, mother of four children with special needs)

At the time of the follow-up meeting, Margaret had just hit one of these crises where her youngest son's school situation had deteriorated and he was at home full time again. Margaret spent the days between trying to help him cope and arranging an alternative school setting together with the multi-disciplinary team. The combination of having 'missed the boat' and mothering four children with special needs is likely to have a negative psychological effect on the mother. Researchers such as Lewis *et al.* have highlighted the psychological benefits for mothers of disabled children to participate in the workforce. Lewis and her colleagues conclude that 'inherent and structural barriers' (1999, p.561) are the main factors preventing mothers of children with special needs from working. The authors recommend various measures in order to provide support to these mothers, such as flexibility in the workplace and integration between health, education and social services. Lewis *et al.* explain their decision to focus on the perspective of the mothers' isolation in combining caring and employment rather than the fathers': 'This was because the fathers interviewed rarely felt the need to justify their employment status in the way that many mothers did, since generally this represented an ideologically accepted "norm"' (1999, p.573). Similarly, in my study, the fathers' employment status was not questioned by the mothers and remained unchanged during the duration of the research (see Chapter 5). Although ten of my participants chose to stay at home and were happy to do so, they did not really have the choice of returning to work. As mentioned earlier, the difficulties in finding people who are capable and willing to mind these children are enormous as special care and knowledge is essential for this type of work.

Work outside the home: a needed income

Two of my participants, Margaret (mother of Jonathan born with Down syndrome and diagnosed ADHD), and Mary (mother of Patrick, diagnosed ADHD), were the main breadwinners in two-parent families and thus had to work for financial reasons (both employees within health boards). They did not have the options of giving up work or moving from full time to part time. Margaret returned to work after three months maternity leave with Jonathan:

> I think if [husband] had been working full-time, I wouldn't have gone back to work at all. But in hindsight I think that would have been a mistake... It was very difficult, I found it very, very difficult for the first, or for a long time. I couldn't afford not to [go back to work] basically. I just did not have the money... I think, you know, if given the choice, I wouldn't have gone back that soon, and I wouldn't have gone back full

> time. At some stage, to have gone back to work, I think, would have been good. (Margaret, mother of Jonathan)

Margaret was relying on her husband to mind Jonathan. Her hours were irregular and he could fit in part-time work around her working schedule. When they both worked, Margaret's mother used to take care of Jonathan. Mary's situation was very similar, her working hours varied from one week to the next, and her husband was involved in casual, part-time work. Likewise, Mary's mother would also mind their son Patrick if both of them worked. Mary had mixed feelings about her full-time job as it gave her 'time for switching off because when I'm with the child I don't switch off', while at the same time it put her under pressure. She would have liked to cut down her hours.

> I had to work financially... I was happy enough to work. I'm in the job like, now what, 22 years, and I would have felt like that I would have thought at this stage, I might have been able to cut down, because there are loads of things now, there's flexi hours and job-sharing... I would have loved to be able to do that, but financially we couldn't. (Mary, mother of Patrick)

Both Margaret and Mary came from working-class backgrounds and, while they were both married, their financial situation depended on them working full time. In my view, these two mothers were faced with a double burden of being responsible for the main family income and at the same time managing all extra tasks involved in mothering a child with special needs (see further discussions in Chapter 5). My findings are similar to several other studies that have been undertaken. Warfield Erickson and Hauser-Cram (1996) researched American mothers of five-year-old children with learning disabilities and found that those who worked full time reported more problems finding childcare compared to those who worked part time, which in turned caused more stress and frustration. Shearn and Todd (2000) similarly conclude that the longer hours the mothers are working the more pronounced are the difficulties trying to manage all extra tasks. Gottlieb (1997) discusses how mothers' lives are negatively affected by stress, depression and health when they are in full-time employment without other important income resources as opposed to when they have partners who also contribute to the income.

Some mothers do not have any choice but are forced financially to go out to work regardless of the quality of care they have for their children. Single mothers of children with special needs have least opportunities and have to balance caregiving and financial demands. They are either in part-time, low-paid jobs with few benefits, or in full-time jobs feeling guilty, considering themselves neglectful of their children's special needs (Gottlieb 1997). Without supportive partners, these single mothers have virtually no time to themselves, as they spend their lives either working or caring for their children.

Having a child with special needs limited the number of hours mothers could spend at work and also their choice of what type of employment they could look for. Two mothers expressed their wish to work full time because of their enjoyment of the actual work or a sense of more time 'free from mothering'. Both Laura (IT-business) and Trish (secretarial work) worked part time, but would have preferred to work more if they were given a choice. Betty (office work) would have worked full time outside home if it was not for her son's disability and she had decided to run a bed and breakfast from home instead.

> Financially, as I got married I had to work...things were tight here, you know. But I would have gone back to work after Michael as well, but sure I couldn't have handled it. (Betty, mother of Michael)

> I worked full time, like I would be working full time if it wasn't for Kevin... I enjoy being at home but I would prefer to be working. I enjoy going out to work, actually, I enjoy the people. (Laura, mother of Kevin)

> I only do two and a half days now, I'm working in a different place, sure, I had to leave loads of jobs over him... I still have my lone parent's book, and then I get 127 [Euro] at work... I'm working to get away from him [laugh] it's not even for the money... I would [work more] but I can't because I have to go to [the] hospital and doctors and whoever on my days off. I make all my appointments on my days off. (Trish, mother of Robert)

In all three cases listed above the mothers gave the lack of appropriate childcare as the main reason why they did not work more hours, although they expressed a wish to do so if they were given a choice. For these mothers employment was an important coping resource. They worked because they wanted to as opposed to financial reasons, a factor also highlighted by other researchers (Baldwin and Carlisle 1994).

Another reason that was given for not being able to work full time was the fact that the mother had to be able to attend numerous appointments with professionals. The issue of not being able to attend meetings with professionals due to full-time employment is addressed in a study conducted in New Zealand (Ballard *et al.* 1997). Interestingly, the authors focus on fathers rather than mothers and their frustration of being left out while 'their wives had to front up to the schools and other professionals involved in meeting their child's needs' (p.239). If this is frustrating for fathers in stereotypical patriarchal families consisting of a breadwinning husband and a housewife, it is easy to understand the increased difficulties occurring where both partners work, or where a lone parent (more than likely a mother) is trying to combine a career and caring for a child with special needs. Again, working mothers face a double burden of both working and taking on the job of negotiating with professionals (see further discussion in Chapter 5).

The option of working from home, such as running a bed and breakfast or minding children, is not available for mothers who have children with behaviour problems. Caitriona, for example, would have liked to mind children in her own home, but due to her son Donnacha's unpredictable behaviour she could not do this. At the time of the first interview Caitriona was working part time for a voluntary organization for minimum wages. This choice of job was a direct result of Caitriona's experience of mothering a child with autism and fighting for appropriate services and she had set up the organization as a support for other parents. However, as Caitriona was relying on fundraising for her minimum wages, this employment situation had a negative financial effect on the family budget.

> If he [Donnacha] had been non-disabled, probably until they [children] were in school, I would probably have stayed at home, but definitely after that I would have done, probably part time, because I would have liked to be at home here when they come home for their dinner. Definitely, or else I would have minded children here, I would have been doing something, whereas by having Donnacha, I couldn't have other kids here because I wasn't sure what way he'd react with them, so it did stop me from having any real income. (Caitriona, mother of Donnacha)

Unlike Caitriona, Therese, mother of John, diagnosed with Asperger syndrome, was able to take on childminding as an extra source of income, as her son's special needs did not interfere with this undertaking. Therese also ran a small-scale, home-based retail business. Her past negative experience as an employee in a large chain store had influenced her choice of work rather than her son's disability.

> They were horrible people to work with, so they kind of added to my misery. I think if I was still at work in that environment...I wouldn't be able to handle John...because I don't work for them anymore, I work for myself...it's brilliant, I mean, I'm not making a fortune or anything like that, but it's still something that I'm doing. (Therese, mother of John)

Therese found satisfaction in being in control over her own business rather than working for an employer. At the follow-up meeting a year later, in conversation with another mother (Anne) who also minded children in her own home, both mothers stated that they had no wish to work full time as they felt that it would be too stressful. During the research process the children of both these mothers were in school full time and had their needs met. This gave the mothers time to do other things than 'mother special needs'. Other mothers in my study had, however, due to various circumstances become full-time teachers for their own children.

Maternal work: becoming a full-time teacher

The maternal work involved in mothering a child with special needs is, as already mentioned, both time consuming and demanding. All 18 participants in my study invested many hours per week dealing with matters relating to their child. Four in particular had dedicated prolonged periods, varying from six months to years, educating their children at home. These mothers were:

1. Miriam, mother of William, born with Down syndrome, who followed an intensive home-programme at the time of the first interview.
2. Helen, mother of Andrew, born with Down syndrome, had taught her son at home for some time before he entered a mainstream school.
3. Julie, mother of John, diagnosed with high-functioning autism, had followed an intensive home-programme for two years with her boy, who at the time of the first interview was in mainstream.
4. Brenda, mother of Susan and Sally, had spent years teaching her two girls at home, preparing them for mainstream education.

> I then felt that this was a way of putting in time when he's much smaller...because he's younger he's far more ready to soak up information than when he's older, so if I put in a lot of effort now, that it would actually save me a lot of effort later on, and hopefully keep him in mainstream all the way through. (Miriam, mother of William)

> I had a lot of material and stuff and I knew what I wanted to do with him. Basically building on what he'd done in the play school, just working with numbers and letters and story time, hand-eye co-ordination, you know, the gross motor and the fine motor movements, that sort of stuff, I mean I just used common stuff that we had in the house, you know, like pasta shapes. (Helen, mother of Andrew)

> I had read about it on the Internet, I said I was going to get this manual, got the manual from the States and set up my own ABA [Applied Behaviour Analysis] programme for John... After nine months I needed more materials, he just...went the rate with knots, the first three months were very, very slow, but he went through that ABA programme with the rate of knots. (Julie, mother of John)

> I went out and got them a computer and just got them a tremendous amount of programmes for every age group, I mean from toddlers, you know, and then we would do things like, I labelled everything in the house, and you just, you kind of learn how to teach these children. (Brenda, mother of Susan and Sally)

These four mothers decided, for the various reasons listed below, that their children would benefit from being taught at home by them. They were all financially capable of devoting themselves to full-time teaching, and more importantly, they shared a willingness and energy to become teachers as well as mothers for a large part of the day. It is of great importance to highlight the financial and personal circumstances that enabled these mothers to make this decision. If the same programmes were made available through the educational system in Ireland, these mothers might have preferred to keep the actual mothering apart from the teaching. So why then did these four mothers choose to become full-time teachers for their children? Miriam did it because she was not convinced that children with Down syndrome had their needs met properly in mainstream and that the special needs school was not a suitable alternative. Consequently, when she came across an intensive parent-led home programme she decided to go for it:

> What came through to me was that the children who went out to mainstream education, and certainly the Down syndrome children, did very well in junior infants, senior infants, first class, and then somewhere, first class or second class they started to fall behind dreadfully...and then...to get to the special school, the children are picked up...depending on where they live, they drive all over all the other estates, collecting, and I mean to be sitting on a bus for an hour there and an hour back in the traffic and then going over to a school where you hear that some of the parents think it's not that nice because there's a series of old buildings and the very young children and the much older children are all in the same complex. (Miriam, mother of William)

Helen approached the mainstream school for her son Andrew when he was five years old, but met with resistance and negative attitudes. The principal would not take him in that September and Helen decided to teach him at home for six months:

> I suppose I could have forced it and insisted that he'd go in. And prompt him in there and do a protest job. But I didn't think that was going to do Andrew any good, really... I actually contacted the chairman of the board of management of the school and we appealed to him...he actually got in touch with her [principal] and she agreed to take him for two days from the following January. (Helen, mother of Andrew)

Both Miriam and Helen experienced difficulties considering the option of sending their boys to mainstream education and their narratives indicate that there is a paradox between reality and statutory policies regarding children with Down syndrome and the educational system in Ireland. During the follow-up interviews (approximately a year later) with these mothers, the vulnerable situation regarding their boys and their respective mainstream school was obvious. Miriam had moved from an urban to a rural area in order to better facilitate William's integration into mainstream education. She felt that the stigma towards learning disabilities was more prominent in the large city and that the local, rural school was more open minded. Miriam herself, however, remained in close contact with her son's school during the day and was on standby should they need her for anything. She felt willing to do this after having been his full-time teacher for several years and knowing how to deal with some of his behaviour problems. Helen expressed her worries regarding Andrew's situation in the school, saying that he seemed unhappy lately. She was also constantly on standby and was prepared to take him home and continue his education should mainstream fail.

Julie and Brenda, both mothers of children with autism, were at the time of the first interview very satisfied with the mainstream school situation. Both Julie's son John and Brenda's girls Susan and Sally had earlier been diagnosed autistic with a severe learning disability and given a bleak prognosis. Julie embarked on an ABA programme at home when she was told that there was no service available for her then four-year-old son:

> I thought I'd be able to go back to work, when I saw, when my 'perfect' boy was born... I thought, yeah, OK, two more years now, I'll stay at home two more years with him and then I'll go back to the bank... They [special pre-school staff] said, look Julie, we've had a meeting about it and we can't really facilitate you. So I said 'alright, OK' and I said 'Can you give me anything to go on with?' and they said 'My heart goes out to you, but he's really taking from the other kids' and I said 'I don't want that, anyhow, if they're making progress'...so anyway, 'Goodbye and Good Luck', so that was it! (Julie, mother of John)

Julie decided not to return to her job as a bank official but to invest her time and energy teaching John at home.

Another mother, Brenda, was living with her two girls in the US at the time her girls Susan and Sally were sent to a public school for children with disabilities at the age of four and three. She recalled this experience as a 'nightmare':

> The conditions in the school were appalling...no windows, no doors, no air-conditioning, no heat, it was basically a closet... and then I found out that she [a teacher] was abusing my daughter... She was jerking her around by her hands and arms, and she would take her to the bathroom and just throw her down on a hard tiled floor, nothing underneath her, in front of all the other children, you know, the bigger kids, and the bigger kids would have to step over her, you know, to go in and out the door, and Susan was so embarrassed and so humiliated that every time she would go in her nappy she would cry and say she was sorry, and I didn't find out about this abuse for...several months, but I knew something wasn't right... so that's when I pulled them out. (Brenda, mother of Susan and Sally)

Brenda taught her girls at home until she decided to move to Ireland, where she had her ancestral roots, and was full of praise of the mainstream school where her girls were placed. They were in a classroom of their own within a mainstream school. They had their own teacher plus one assistant each. Prior to moving here she had also asked for a renewed psychological assessment, which confirmed that the girls no longer had autism with severe learning disabilities, but had made so much progress they were now considered having Asperger syndrome.

> I mean it's been just absolutely brilliant since I've had them here...like I said, we progressed slowly in America but I wasn't qualified to teach these children, I was basically tramping water, you know, and doing my best, but we were still going forward, but since we came here, I mean the pace of their progress has just picked up enormously. (Brenda, mother of Susan and Sally)

Susan and Sally were nine and eight when they started in their mainstream school in Ireland, having left the American public pre-school five years previously. Brenda was very satisfied that her girls' educational needs were perfectly met in Ireland and she had no regrets leaving her native country.

Julie, however, had not the same praise to give to the Irish educational system a year and a half after our initial meeting. Her son John had also made enormous progress during the years Julie taught him at home, and was academically well able to follow the mainstream curriculum. Julie, however, felt that the government's cutbacks were now beginning to affect the support for children with special needs, and that authorities were now questioning John's original diagnosis as severely autistic.

> In the year of the Disabled People, the cutbacks are coming...and that is going to affect John's education too...six years ago he was diagnosed with autism and severe learning disability, and with that label he was entitled to a classroom assistant and resource teaching. Now the inspector asks 'Aren't we looking at Asperger's here?' (Julie, mother of John)

Both Julie and her husband were delighted that John had made such fantastic progress but were also furious that a change in diagnosis should be made only to suit the Minister for Finance who, according to them, is cutting down services for children with special needs. Some 18 months after the initial meeting with Julie, communications between John and his teacher had broken down completely and Julie was again teaching John at home.

The cases mentioned above (Brenda and Julie) highlight the importance of 'maternal work' in cases where a child with autism has been 'written off' by professionals. These mothers were given a negative picture of their children's conditions without appropriate support. Julie was given no alternative but to take her child home again and Brenda had the choice of leaving her girls in an inappropriate environment or taking them home. Both Julie and Brenda decided to spend years intensively teaching their own children and were rewarded by the progress the children made. The private and personal fulfilment of these mothers was evident in the narratives.

> I'd go down that road again with John, because there's nothing like the, I know other mothers don't get the feelings I get, because everything he does now is a bonus... I'm glad in my own particular case because he has made such progress. (Julie, mother of John)

> And these children have opened up my eyes, so that I see things differently, so I've gained as much from them as I've given. (Brenda, mother of Susan and Sally)

Nevertheless, the financial reward for this work in the private sphere remained absent for these mothers. Julie was fortunate to have a breadwinning spouse, whereas Brenda's financial situation as a single, unemployed mother remained vulnerable.

> Their dad has to pay child support, and we get child maintenance which I will continue to get until the shop starts making a profit, I mean enough profit to support us... and then I'm getting the [Domiciliary Care Allowance] you know, so that will make a difference, so financially it'll work out, but I tell you what – it's been an experience. I mean living on nothing [laugh] but you do what you have to do, especially if you're doing it for your children. (Brenda, mother of Susan and Sally)

Since arriving in Ireland, Brenda started making plans for herself again and hoped to set up a bookstore. However, her situation depended on the continued support from the girls' school and other service providers. The volatile situation facing children with special needs attending mainstream schools has a negative effect on the mothers' careers. At least 4 of the 18 mothers were on constant standby should the school need help in managing their children. The mothers' expertise, from this point of view, was seen as invaluable support, however 'hidden' and unpaid by the state.

Maternal work: extraordinary support

The mothers whose children had always been full time in the educational system, either in a mainstream school or in a special school, had put in many hours helping their children in various ways depending on their special needs. This took the form of, for example, speech therapy, social skills training and homework. Mary, single mother of her adopted son Donal, diagnosed with Asperger syndrome, spent years doing speech therapy with Donal outside his school hours:

> All I was doing, and seemed to be doing all the time was speech therapy work with him… I couldn't work at the time because I would have to go to his school, as he was in [special school], bring him out to school, and bring him to his speech therapy… And I suppose…I was going to make Donal OK, you know, I had this mission, and I was going to do whatever it took and I did it and it was going to be this year, and then it was going to be the next year…I was going to do it. But I felt, other than the speech therapist, I was working on my own, and that's how it felt, I felt really left out, you know. (Mary, mother of Donal)

At the time of the first interview, Mary was working part time in a community employment scheme, but she was also reading up on Asperger syndrome, as Donal had just recently been diagnosed. She was looking for other ways of helping him getting over his difficulties, and she was also trying to find a secondary school that would take him the following year. Mary felt that she had spent years helping her son and that she hoped to return to college herself:

> Once the secondary school is decided, yes or no or whatever, I feel September from this year, I want it to be about me, for a change. I want to do something for me that will get me a career. (Mary, mother of Donal)

A year later, at the follow-up meeting, Donal had started secondary school with the help of a personal assistant and got on very well, according to Mary. She too had started college, but had to give it up after the first term due to unforeseen personal circumstances. She felt that Donal was still in great need of her support and in order to give him that, she could not take on the task of studying full time. Mary's decision to cease her university studies consequently deprived her of pursuing a career and getting a 'life of her own'.

One recurring statement in the interviews with these mothers was that if the mother did not do the extra work involved such as teaching the child nobody else would do it.

> I realize if I don't do anything, if I don't keep on top of it, nobody is going to do it. So I just got to do it. (Mary, mother of Donal)

> I work with him all the time really...social stuff I do with him, I suppose I do it constantly... and if I didn't, where would he be, you know, there's no one else. It's a full-time job. (Mary, mother of Kevin)

> [I]f I had gone out to work, what would have become of my son? I'm giving him an intensive ABA programme at home and they [service provider] basically don't care. (Julie, mother of John)

> Because if you have a child like that, even if it's not your personality, you have to force yourself to do it. Because you think that he can't do it for himself, I'm his mother, like if I'm not going to do it, who is going to do it? (Margaret, mother of Jonathan)

Mary's son, Kevin, diagnosed with Asperger syndrome, was doing very well academically in his mainstream school but had great difficulties in socializing and relating to peers. Mary had spent many long and hard hours trying to teach him skills like riding a bicycle and climbing gates, skills that non-disabled children learn naturally:

> [I]t takes an enormous amount of perseverance and the teacher just doesn't have the time, you know, so I have to do it. No matter what she does, I have to do it at home as well...another thing I taught him was...he didn't know how to climb, you know, another person would find that unbelievable that a child didn't know how to climb, he didn't know to put one foot up and keep climbing so I took him one day, you know, to a field where nobody could see us, with a gate and I had him climbing back and forth over the gate until he learnt how to climb it, I mean if anyone saw me they'd think I was absolutely out of my mind, but these are the things that I have to do. (Mary, mother of Kevin)

The lack of understanding of how much hard work is involved in mothering a child with special needs seemed to be particularly felt by the mothers of children with Asperger syndrome who got on very well academically in mainstream schools:

> [N]obody knows and you're told 'oh, you're so lucky your children are so intelligent and they don't know what's gone in to try and get them to do their homework with chairs being kicked all over the place and it takes

> four hours to do half an hour's work and that you're listening to...these ridiculous conversations all day to drive you around the bend, if it's not dinosaurs it's aliens and that. (Margaret, mother of four)

Fighting for services: another full-time job

Apart from mothering a child with a learning disability, the mother also faces the time-consuming task of fighting for services for her child. This extra work is unwelcome and very often causes more stress and frustration amongst these women. All my 18 participants had spent many hours making phone calls and chasing professionals over the years. One mother had gone to court in order to get her child a place in a school:

> [W]hen the department still hadn't found a place for him I said, that's it, I'm taking it to court. So in May of that year, when he was four, the case was in court and a place was found for him... I was just so exhausted and then I'd leave it for a while, and then you'd get a spurt of energy, so I thought I had nothing else, I mean I had gone every avenue, you know, knocked at every door, politicians...sent pictures of Donnacha, no answer, you know, brought Donnacha to all these politicians and still got no answer from them, it was terrible. (Caitriona, mother of Donnacha)

Going down the road of litigation was seen as the last option for mothers as it was time consuming and stressful. During the time of the research process, Caitriona was the only mother in my study who had gone through the courts in order to get help. Other mothers relied on politicians to assist them in their struggle and waited patiently, albeit prepared to fight if needed:

> I remember being horrified when I saw the building because the then Minister of Education came to see it...and open it and I remember thinking is he not shocked that six little boys started school in...basically in a shed? Would they not have better facilities in Romania? And he obviously wasn't, because he cut the ribbon and we had tea and scones and everyone celebrated, looking back I don't know what the hell we were celebrating because it was awful, I remember my heart sinking thinking is this it? But it was it. But I had to go along with it because at least then we were in a system and I thought, well I'll make the system suit me, it'll have to get better... We were always fighting really, because we fought even to get him, I mean I had to go to a government minister...just even to get him into [service provider] because some of the parents had actually gone to court even to get their kids into some system which was

> obviously causing a bit of shake up in [service provider]. (Marie, mother of Eoin)

Marie chose the strategy of accepting a sub-standard educational service for her son Eoin, but only as a temporary solution and her involvement in the parent-led campaign eventually paid off. A year later Eoin started in a special school designed to meet his needs. Marie's struggle, however, did not end there. Lack of respite was next on her agenda as the service provider only offered two days every ten weeks: 'we even visited the Minister of Health about it [but] there's nothing coming up'. Another mother, Mary, had also geared herself up for a battle concerning the lack of respite and shared care:

> I plan to get all that we can, to get all the support, help and what's right in hours and what's suitable, what is Patrick's needs and what's appropriate to him in his care and support system... I feel that I've made noise and I want to continue to make noise, they know that I'm not going away, they know my face with the past eight years, certainly seven years anyway, and that I'm certainly not going to be taken back down. (Mary, mother of Patrick)

A year after the initial interview Mary had contacted a solicitor and with the help of his letter she managed to pressurize the service provider to increase the hours in respite for her son. Instead of two days every ten weeks, he spent every second weekend in respite, which gave Mary and her family a chance to have a quality time together.

Another mother, Martina, had also seriously considered legal action when endless phone calls proved fruitless in trying to secure speech therapy for her son. She abandoned the idea, however, as she got a place in college with the aim of becoming a speech therapist herself:

> I figured, well, I can look after him myself, and when I look after him I'm gonna look, you know, I hope to help other kids...because I've given up on the state, I think it's just, it's just terrible... I'm really disgusted with it and there's no support and you ring places and 'oh, we're going to help' and 'you'll get this and you'll get that' but you're just fobbed off all the time. (Martina, mother of Daniel)

Like Martina, many other mothers in my research felt they wasted time and energy in a hopeless struggle for appropriate services such as speech therapy and allowances. Making phone calls, writing letters, visiting local politicians' clinics and embarking on court cases – the list is endless, the hours are countless and the result is often nothing:

> It [health board-run speech therapy] was really a waste of time…but you knew you had to do it, and you knew you had to go along, because if you wanted something in the future, somewhere along…so they give you the time and you go along and take the time, so it was like a total disruption whatever was happening, you know, because you had to fit it with their time. (Miriam, mother of William)

> I was applying for this Domiciliary Care Allowance, you know, as yet I haven't heard a word…but what happened was, didn't they lose my form, so that's how, and I rang, so I've been ringing kind of every week. (Therese, mother of John)

> I wrote to the head of the services…and no reply, this is over a year ago…nothing, and I called the office a few times and I got absolutely no reply. I just wanted to see was there any services available. Not that I had been told that there was anyway. (Marie, mother of Kevin)

Other mothers had a more militant attitude describing their efforts to make sure their children's needs were met:

> The other thing was the Domiciliary Allowance then, the very first thing she [medical doctor] said: 'Well, you have to bring the child here and that's reviewed every year' and I think the very first thing she said to me was 'This isn't, you can't backdate this now!' so straight away you're made to feel you're looking for something and you're not entitled to it. It's horrible, it's absolutely horrible! But I didn't care at that stage, in a way, I'm glad that it was at that stage that I found out about it, because I would not have been strong enough earlier on to deal with the looks and the comments and I would have just burst into tears and ran away… But at that stage I did not give a shit. I thought, this is my entitlement and you're failing him in enough ways, you know… For goodness sake! So I got that, but it took a while to get that kind of pigheadedness into me. (Julie, mother of John)

> So then you take on the fighting of the system. You're not wrecked enough before this, you're not totally fecked up as a family, and then you start with the system. (Mary, mother of Patrick)

> I would always had kind of stood up and fought for what I kind of believed in, but probably more so now, because I'm probably doing a lot more of that...and I would have fought for things for them [other children] as well if I felt they were being wrong or victimized or whatever, but I suppose I wouldn't have had to do as much of that. Very little, really, I would say, you know...you do have the hassle then with fighting for services and fighting for this. (Margaret, mother of Jonathan)

> [T]hey sort of don't want to know you when you go to mainstream, sure they don't, sure there's no help, there's no finance. I've asked and rang and looked and whatever, but never got anything... I ended up having to really fight hard. (Betty, mother of Michael)

The terms 'fight' and 'battle' are frequently used by the participants: 'It wasn't just a battle, it was a war' (Betty); 'the battle is on' (Helen). These warlike statements highlight how they perceived this particular task being added on to their daily workload. Furthermore, it is one that with proper services in place could have been avoided. In this limited research, the mothers involved were resilient and determined to keep up the struggle. However, where circumstances are different and mothers have other, more urgent, worries such as poverty, domestic violence or alcohol abuse, it is easy to understand that they do give up and accept whatever is handed to them. As a consequence these women's lives become very restricted and their hard work goes on unnoticed.

More importantly, many mothers lost out financially when they gave up their paid employment:

> So eventually anyway, we got the Domiciliary Care Allowance...at the time I think it was £129 or something like that [per month]...in my job I was coming out with £600 a month. (Anne, mother of Noel)

> I still have my lone parent's book and then I get £127 at work, so like it does, to make up for it. That's towards childcare and all that kind of thing...you see, I don't drink and I don't smoke and I don't go out. So I don't do anything really. (Trish, mother of Robert)

Anne's subdued reaction to an income drop of almost £500 per month and Trish's acceptance of living on minimum finances revealed that money was not their greatest worry. It was instead the education and services for their children. Contributing to a relatively 'placid' attitude towards financial compensation, apart from the mother's sheer lack of time and energy, is the cultural environment in which these women are living. Mothering is very much taken for granted as an unpaid prescribed role for women in society, whether the child is non-disabled or not. One mother reacted strongly against this assumption:

> We're discriminated against in the home... They're now talking about the new relief on crèches and tax relief...but nobody's asking the question 'What about the people who simply cannot work?' or those people who are going out to work because it's going to be childcare, but rather not. They should all have the option of staying at home. I mean, it's not if people are stuck to stay at home for ever and ever, because in a normal functioning family, you could take time off and actually start going back slowly and you're still there for the kids after school, you know, I think people aren't looking at the whole picture. (Margaret, mother of four children with ASD)

Margaret, who had mothered children with special needs for nearly two decades and as a consequence left her career behind, wanted society to recognize and financially reward her maternal work in the home. One election year, Margaret took the opportunity to confront a politician who canvassed for her vote:

> He [the politician] was on my doorstep last night, I talked to him, Andrew was screaming, Andrew was hyper, and I said: 'Did you hear that?' And he said: 'Yes'. And I said: 'Well, I have four of that...you've got four kids, but your wife is able to work. Would you work with that?' And he just said: 'No.' And I said: 'Charlie McCreevy [Minister for Finance] expects me to go out with that. Who would mind them?' I mean, at this stage Andrew was getting worse, he couldn't have timed it better, and he said: 'No, you couldn't, nobody would mind them.' (Margaret, mother of four)

However, in the era of the Celtic Tiger where Ireland is booming economically, the government is anxious to get mothers back into employment. This was particularly evident in the Budget of 2006, where families with children under the age of six were given an allowance of 1,000 euros per child per year as an attempt to solve the current childcare crisis (O'Brien 2005a). There are few political efforts, however, to financially support mothers of children with special needs either at home or to return to paid employment. It is perhaps not surprising then that many of these women choose to work voluntarily in the disability sector in order to support others in the same situation.

Extended care in the wider community

Mothers of children with special needs often choose a career within the field of learning disabilities. This involvement has been documented as a third concept of caring, where mothers add the task of caring for people in the wider community to their already heavy workload of caring for and caring about their own children (Traustadottir 1991). They do this by becoming active within support groups or by educating themselves further in the field of learning disabilities. All of my 18 participants were members of various support groups related to their child's disability. Sixteen of them had joined or approached organizations to get support from other parents and to gain more information. Nine of the mothers were active members, including two mothers who initiated and formed their own organizations.

> I did informally first [set up a support group for parents]. There was another girl and the two of us said we'd love to meet other parents, you know, so we put an ad in the paper...we started meetings once a month then. (Laura, mother of Kevin)

Despite initial support from other parents the involvement sometimes added to feelings of stress and disappointment:

> All I wanted was just to help other people who were maybe going through a similar situation or to make sure that nobody ever went through what I went through and that's why I started it up [parents' support group] and if anything, it has caused terrible trouble here with phone calls at all hours of the day and night, you know. We find now that new parents coming onboard are not as needy cause they have the Internet and all that kind of thing, whereas we had nothing and I think that maybe that was the hunger to begin with. (Caitriona, mother of Donnacha)

Caitriona worked part time for this group, but doubted if all the hard work she had put into her organization, such as spending hours on the phone trying to support other parents, was really worth her effort. In doing all this, she had neglected herself and her needs, and she felt bitter about not getting more practical help from other parents:

> I'm mentally and physically exhausted but I still have to drive my 20 miles or whatever to the meeting. It's not a good enough excuse to say that I'm not able... It's your child we're talking about here, and it shouldn't be me fighting for your child. (Caitriona)

Paradoxically, Julie rejected becoming active in a support group because she only had energy to focus on her own child:

> [T]hat other mum said to me 'sometimes Julie, you were blindfolded in one way – John, John, John'. John got every single thing. But I did, and I apologize to no one for that... I know there has to be the Kathy Sinnotts of this world too, but I just wasn't one. I wouldn't be able, no way would I be strong enough. I knew my own capabilities and I thought, right, if I just make it right for him...but I couldn't spread myself anymore than I was already doing. (Julie, mother of John)

Julie spent two years teaching John intensively at home and as a result had very little time and energy to become active within existing support networks.

Similarly, Miriam felt pressure from another mother who urged her to share her 'private' teaching of her son with others:

> She was sort of like attacking me for doing this and it was like if this was the answer...why wasn't I out there telling everyone? And I was sort of saying, I can't do that, I'm just, I'm here, I have to concentrate on my own child now, and like, if I do something else later, if it's a success, I'll tell somebody about that. (Miriam, mother of William)

Julie and Miriam are examples of mothers who chose to spend energy individually rather than in a wider campaign. As a consequence of that decision they both experienced the group dynamic as negative and unhelpful.

Three other participants, Margaret, Marie and Helen, similarly felt that support groups added to their own misery rather than the opposite:

> I've taken part in support groups and I find that groups don't really suit me. Because sometimes I feel that I come out, having heard all the very different stories of people and having taken some of these onboard and I find it quite upsetting...maybe it's selfish...but I feel I have enough problems on my own. (Marie, mother of Eoin)

> I don't intend to stay going [to a support group] for ever because you could just end up being very depressed, but I think a couple of sessions initially to share ideas and to find out what's happening...but I can't see myself keep going because you just get bogged down in other people's problems. (Margaret, mother of four with ASD)

> I was the chairman last year and I resigned because of the stupidity that was going on... My own personal feeling is that there's a clique in the

> organization, and really, they're involved in things that concern themselves. And basically, they're not, it's not an outward looking group. (Helen, mother of Andrew)

One mother, Mary, had a negative experience of being involved in a planning group on respite organized by the service provider:

> I was a representative from the parents' pressure group attending it...you're talking about seven–eight people sitting around the table. I couldn't tell you the length of time I went and attended that but it was, I'd say, basically six months or more...the huge effort that went into that, but it amounted to zero. I actually saw the plans for the building at one stage... I don't know what it fell on, we were never told... The whole thing fell through and it wasn't going ahead. And I suppose as parents we didn't have to be accounted to, they didn't feel they owed us an apology... I felt very used and I still do, having been brought onboard there and given...your insight and pouring your heart out and giving your input and working hard on it. (Mary, mother of Patrick)

Mary's involvement in the service provider's planning group was a positive step forward to a potential partnership between parents and professionals. However, when it came to the crucial decision of implementing suggested services, Mary was powerless. Her input had, according to her, been a waste of time and had not improved her personal situation at all. The service provider's lack of finances once again left her, and other service users, facing a future full of uncertainties.

Mothering special needs: a never ending job?

A striking finding from the participants' narratives was that their view to the future had very little to do with their own personal fulfilment, but was all closely connected to their child with special needs. When asked about where they saw themselves in ten years' time, the focus was on where the child was: 'I think Patrick will be here for the rest of his life, somehow or other. I get that impression, you know, because he's a real home bird' (Mary, mother of Patrick).

> Ideally, I would love to think of him being able to have his own house and budget things and...I'm a bit worried about that, I must say that does worry me...unless he gets huge help with social skills, and I don't think I

> can see him doing that for a long, long time. If ever. If ever actually. He could be living with me for the rest of his life. (Mary, mother of Donal)

> I'll be there for him as long as it takes, do you know what I mean? I'd prefer if he never got married either, I'd prefer if he stayed at home with me, so I could always look after him, but I don't know is that possible. (Therese, mother of John)

> He would have to be watched like, I suppose like, by me, I suppose he'd be very vulnerable. (Trish, mother of Robert)

The four mothers above seemed to be resigned to the fact that their children with special needs would be living at home with them forever. They were worried about their lack of social skills and felt that they would always be in need of extra help. They were of the opinion that there was only one person able to provide this support: the mother. In these particular cases, some factors might have contributed to this uncertain sense of 'endless' mothering. First, the children were high functioning (ADHD and Asperger syndrome) and would all have been integrated in mainstream society with its potential risks for vulnerable people. Second, the children were still relatively young (in primary school) and it was hard to predict their potential at this early stage. The mothers were, however, worried about the transition to secondary school:

> What's ahead of Noel when he goes to secondary school? Because a child like Noel, if he goes to a normal secondary school, he's going to be left in the back of the classroom, and he'll be either a bully or he'll be bullied… I would be more depressed over it because I think the road ahead is not going to be easy. (Anne, mother of Noel)

Anne also worried about Noel's future as an adult: 'Noel to go out and live independently would probably be my biggest nightmare… I would be constantly worried about him.' While reflecting a bit more over this 'maternal' worry, Anne also argued that mothers of all children, special needs or not, always worry about them and that the worry she had for her son was not that much different. Other mothers would agree with her on that point:

> I don't look too far into the future concerning my two other sons, so, you know, almost why should I do it about him? In one sense, I don't want to, even, he's part of our lives, he's not the main focus of our lives. My one concern, I suppose, would be that he would not become the responsibil-

> ity of [his older brothers] that's the only thing, or that they wouldn't feel that they would have to take him on. (Helen, mother of Andrew)

Although Helen did not want to focus on Andrew in particular regarding the future at that moment in time, she acknowledged the fact that he would require extra support as an adult. Helen's hope was that his brothers would not have to be responsible for that task.

Betty, mother of Michael, also born with Down syndrome, felt the same:

> It's not their responsibility [older daughters] that Michael has Down syndrome, but I'd like to think that we'd have our affairs in order that there be so much put there for Michael, or even, let's say, the long term, I'd like even that they lived in residential care or something, you know. (Betty, mother of Michael)

Betty visualized Michael living in some form of residential care eventually. One of her daughters, however, insisted that Michael would remain with her on the farm as she took it over from her parents, despite Betty's objection: 'I still don't want them to have to feel that they have to take Michael, that day is gone, isn't it, where you married somebody and you took [care of a relation]'. Proper residential care, a home away from home, was also considered by Marie, whose son Eoin would always need high support due to his severe learning disability:

> In my mind Eoin will remain with us here until he's 18, as any child you hope would...and after 18 that he might have a residential place, but even part time, you know, and that it would be as nice as his home, or nicer, and have all the facilities that he needs, not something like a hospital. (Marie, mother of Eoin)

Marie was sadly aware that this type of residential unit did not exist and the chances of it ever materializing were slim considering poor services for people with disabilities (see Chapter 2). Unless there was a dramatic change in service provisions, Eoin would therefore more than likely remain at home with Marie, whose mothering would continue as long as she was able.

So where then, within this pessimistic future scenario, did these mothers see themselves? Most of them recognized their own need for an outlet but it did not necessarily involve bringing in money:

> I needed an outlet, instead of going out earning money I'm out spending it now [laugh]. But no, to be serious, I suppose, I just, I am a person that

> needs to do things outside the home...very much, I need to be involved in groups, I need to be doing stuff. I just need to find things, especially when this is my time during the year. I devote myself totally, well, we all do, to our kids, but summer time when my husband is away working, with Patrick in summer school and keeping the others going, I think when September comes, that's always been my time to, to settle down and do my night classes, and I have the kids back to the routine of school and to me that's almost like having a part-time job without the wages. (Mary, mother of Patrick)

In September, with the children returning to school, the mothers could afford to think of themselves to a certain extent. As already mentioned in this chapter, returning to college was seen as an outlet for some of my participants: Mary, mother of Donal, Martina, mother of Daniel and Margaret, mother of Jonathan. Paradoxically, this engagement prevented them further from having any time for leisure and hobbies:

> I don't at the moment do anything [for myself] because I have so much to do. I have college, and I just feel when the college is finished now, then maybe I might have time. But that has really been my outlet for the last two years. (Margaret, mother of Jonathan)

All my 18 participants felt that their time for leisure and social activities was extremely limited as the bulk of their time awake was spent between mothering their child and, in some cases, engaging in employment or studies. This lack of freedom was, however, hardly ever seen as a sacrifice. On the contrary, the unselfishness of the mother was portrayed as a virtue and sometimes as an alternative to materialistic thinking:

> I sold all my antiques, all my furniture, my dishes, my pottery, everything...27 years of my life went out the front door, and I didn't even have any regrets then, and up until then I had been, I wouldn't say I'm a materialistic person, but my home was very important, but now I'm faced with two autistic children. (Brenda, mother of Susan and Sally)

> I still teach yoga one night a week, and I find I lost touch with...a lot of people are working, a lot of mothers are working now anyway... What are we here on this earth for...you know, is it to earn lots of money, is it to, you know, knit beautiful things, is it to paint paintings? I felt a yearning to go back to [career] but now everything is more of a conscious effort to do that...when you're doing all this [teaching child at home]

> you have no time or energy for anything else. None for anything else, and when you do have extra time it's like to take care of all the household things, instead of sort of let go. (Miriam, mother of William)

'Letting go' is something that is very hard to do for a mother of a child with special needs and it can only be done when the mother is reassured that the child is taken care of satisfactorily and is making progress. Thus, the mother's happiness is again closely connected to the child's wellbeing:

> And, you know, I just gave up on feeling guilty not having enough time to devote to Patrick, I was going to feel guilty for the rest of my life, because I was never going to be able to give him all the time he needed. And that's where the home support and the extra bit of help comes in. I'm much happier because I know Patrick is getting it, and I know it's stuff Patrick loves and he's enjoying it and he's also progressing with this bit of support. And I don't think I'd be able to do it as well as the girls, because I would be, I'd be under more stress. (Mary, mother of Patrick)

Mary looked positively to the future, believing that her son Patrick would receive the care she wanted him to get, albeit with a lot of fighting for the same.

Catriona felt similarly about her son Donnacha and aimed to obtain autism specific residential care for him. Nevertheless, Catriona emphasized that this was not done to 'get rid of him':

> I don't want to, as I said, when he's at home and when he's good, he's a pleasure, it's just when he's bad, you know, it's exhausting, and it's not getting rid of him, it's just getting a break, that's the way I'm looking at it. Now other parents would say, oh, they've no social life and stuff, it wouldn't affect me if I never went out again, it's just a bit of peace. (Caitriona, mother of Donnacha)

All my participants refused the notion that these children with special needs had to be 'gotten rid of' one way or another, either by themselves as mothers or by society at large.

> I'd like to see a more inclusive society…to see everybody with worth in society without 'where are we going to get rid of the person'… I think to be out in society and for society just to know, that everybody just doesn't have to be, you know, need to be more efficient every day. (Miriam, mother of William)

One very important part of the maternal work undertaken by the mothers became one where they worked towards this inclusion and acceptance by society. Brenda, for example, hoped that the hard work she spent in training her two girls Susan and Sally would pay off in the future:

> Ten years from now they will be working in that bookstore, getting prepared to take it over, cause that's my long term goal...the whole purpose of it being a bookstore, is because I think it is the one thing that they'll be able to do, they might need a manager or an accountant, but they can go in and weigh down the paper, they can stack the shelves, they can order the books, and they've got ten years to learn that, and then they won't feel like they're different or life on the dole or they're outcasts, they'll be a little different, but they're gonna be productive and they're gonna be respected. What more can you ask from anybody? (Brenda, mother of Susan and Sally)

Judging from the quotes above, the maternal thinking that is involved to 'protect, nurture and train' children (Ruddick 1989, p.23) and which manifests itself in the actual work that the mothers do, seemed to remain strongly also in their thinking of the future. In this sense, these mothers will never let go, but remain by their children's side forever. Surprisingly, this was not considered as a serious problem at this point of time in the mothers' lives. The relatively young ages of the children could perhaps explain why they did not worry too much about the future, but focused on 'here and now' instead. As Trish, mother of Robert, diagnosed ADHD, responded when asked about how she felt about 'mothering' her son as a grown up man: 'I never thought of it that way, no, I don't think of it that way.'

Conclusion

Having a child with a learning disability will affect the mother's own personal life in many different ways. Most importantly, her choice of having a career outside the home is extremely limited due to lack of adequate childcare services and educational provisions. The majority of the mothers in this book had ceased their employment outside the home, or cut down their work hours, in order to provide extra support for their children. In this limited study many of the mothers looked favourably upon this choice, as it gave them an opportunity to help their children reach their potential. The majority of the mothers staying at home full time (9 out of 10) had breadwinning partners whose incomes were high enough to provide a good quality of life for the whole family. Some of them also had other children and would have chosen to stay at home regardless of one child's disability, in particular while the children were small. Thus, the gender divisions in these families were similar to families with non-disabled children in Ireland (McCarthy 1995).

Although some of my participants claimed to be at home 'by choice' they would have found it very difficult to choose to do otherwise. Those mothers who had to work for financial reasons, or who wanted to work for their own self-fulfilment, found it very hard to do so for several reasons. First, lack of suitable childcare was seen as the largest obstacle for mothers who attempted to work outside the home. The general lack of state-subsidized childcare limits the choices Irish women have as regards combining motherhood and a career (Kennedy 2002). They rely on private crèches and Montessori schools until the child reaches school age. Families who can afford it employ private childminders, au pairs and nannies to take care of the children after school hours and during holidays. Families living with children with learning disabilities, however, experience enormous problems recruiting these child-minders as most lack the knowledge and skills necessary to care for these children. Two of my participants, Anne and Trish, had gone through several childminders who had given up and left due to their children's difficult behaviours. Anne eventually decided to give up her employment, as it made life easier for the whole family. Trish, a single mother, was forced to work only part time, although she would have preferred to work for longer hours. She spent her days off meeting professionals involved in services for her son.

A second reason preventing mothers from participating in the workforce was the amount of time spent meeting professionals and service providers. These meetings took place during working hours and the only way the mother could attend these meetings was if she had flexible conditions at work or did not work outside the home at all. This, so far, has not really been a problem in Ireland, as mothers have generally been available for meetings during the day (Redmond 1993). However, as more and more Irish women are participating in the workforce, this will become more of an issue also here. The pressure of working full time for mothers of children with special needs is also well documented (Gottlieb 1997; Shearn and Todd 2000) and confirmed in this book. Two of the participants, whose full-time employment was the main source of income for the family, expressed a wish to cut down the work hours as they felt under too much pressure to combine this work with mothering a child with special needs. Flexible working hours and partners in part-time or casual employment enabled these two mothers to remain at work full time. Interestingly, the added workload of fighting for services was no less for these two mothers than for the mothers who stayed at home full time. They were still the main advocates in their children's lives, despite the fact that their partners spent more time at home (see next chapter for the discussion of the fathers' involvement).

One important conclusion that can be drawn from the mothers' narratives is that employment outside the home in itself will not emancipate and empower this group of marginalized women in our society. Similarly, disability researcher Paul Abberley criticizes the notion that work is the 'defining characteristic of full social inclusion' (2002, p.120) for all individuals with disabilities. Abberley calls for a new vision within social theory, drawing from certain feminist approaches, where a dual strategy facilitates work for those who want to and values the lives of people who are unable to work. This new way of thinking can also be used in the argument for revaluing the 'maternal work' done by mothers of children with special needs. An inclusive society, therefore, would equally value mothers who cannot work or do not want to work due to the needs of their children as well as mothers who share the 'mothering' with others in order to participate in the workforce.

The maternal work invested by the participating mothers was highly time and energy consuming. Four of my participants had become full-time teachers for their children, for periods varying from six months to several years. They made this decision when state-run services were inadequate or did not exist at all. Relying on information obtained through the Internet or other sources, these mothers pursued intensive programmes in order to help their children reach their full potential and found this very fulfilling. This unpaid work, however, took a heavy toll on these women who sacrificed their own time and energy until they were on the verge of exhaustion. These families were also worse off financially as a consequence of the mothers ceasing paid employment. Furthermore, as documented by other researchers (Read 1991) instead of supporting these mothers financially and psychologically, the state ignored their input and added to their misery by forcing them to struggle and fight for additional services. All participating mothers had experienced a 'battle' or a 'fight' with professionals and service providers at some stage. This added negative workload entailed spending hours on the phone, lobbying politicians and negotiating with service providers. Many of my participants felt that these efforts very often proved fruitless and were generally a waste of time. Despite this sense of hopelessness, the mothers showed extraordinary strength and were determined to get the services that they were entitled to.

Regardless of whether or not mothers worked full time with the child or participated in the workforce, my participants were left with very little time to think or do something for themselves. This did not, however, seem to concern them, as the most important issue in their lives was their children, both at present and while discussing the future. The mother's life was so intertwined with that of the child that plans for her future automatically transferred to that of her child. Thus, whatever the child was doing in 10 years' time would determine the life of the mother. In some cases the mothers saw themselves caring for their children until they were no longer able to do so. Increased support, such as childcare and respite care, would enable mothers of children with special needs to do something for themselves, not necessarily engage in employment outside the home if they do not wish to do so. With appropriate help and a professional understanding of their children's needs, these mothers would be able to let go and share their mothering with other people. This, however, requires an increased awareness regarding gender divisions within families. Both mothers and fathers and society in general, will have to challenge the social construction of motherhood. This challenge will be discussed in the next chapter dealing with the mothers' relationship with the fathers, the extended families and other networks.

Chapter 5

Mothers' Relationships with Fathers, Families and Social Networks

> The maternal thinking is different, it's needed and he's not great organising the house, he's just a typical man.
>
> (Margaret, mother of four children with special needs)

This chapter focuses on the mothers' experiences regarding their relationships with the fathers as well as with their immediate and extended families. It also explores their views on faith and religion and the cultural context in which they are living. I begin by discussing the role of the father and the mother's view on existing gender divisions within their relationship. I move on to discuss the impact having a child with a learning disability has on other siblings in the family and how the mother deals with this situation. Finally, this chapter will discuss the mother's experience of relationships with the extended family and society in general.

The father: the second carer

Of the 18 mothers contributing to this book, 15 were married and 3 were single at the time of the first interview. One year later, at the time of the follow-up meeting, one mother had reunited with the child's father and was living with him again. The mothers' experiences of the support of the father and his role in helping the child with special needs varied from high praise to subtle complaints of lack of understanding.

> [My husband] is very, very positive, very positive... While I sourced everything on the Internet and I did the running, in no way now could I have done that without a man who every Friday and Saturday night... [drove John to a therapist]...anything for the boys, if, you know, if bringing them to the North Pole would make them. Never once did I hear the man say 'Julie, I had a hard day today and I could do without this', so without that, you have nothing. He'll never go on the computer, he'll never read a book about it...he knows nothing about autism, but he knows John inside out. (Julie, mother of John)

> The situation is probably the same in most families. Dad is out working, he's away a lot, but he is the role model, having a lot of fun when he comes home to the kids, which is important for the boys. Father is the great fun and he can switch off while he's at work. He gets his support there, while I do a lot of worrying here at home about the future. He is a great support now and I would hate to do this alone. (Martina, mother of Daniel)

Both Julie and Martina, while acknowledging that they did the 'running' and the 'worrying', felt that they could not do this without the support from the fathers. The important role of the father in the lives of the children was also emphasized by other mothers:

> Well, our [husband and her] worlds are entirely different. I'm at home with the children all day, by choice, and I would be more tuned in, I think, to their needs, and to where they're at, and to things that concern them... My husband, I believe, has an equally important role to play in the family. The boys idolize him. As soon as Dad arrives they 'Ohhhh, Dad is home!' and there's an explosion from the table. And they run out and there's hugs and kisses. (Helen, mother of Andrew)

> William absolutely adores [father] and would do anything for [father] and just wait for [father] to come home and idolizes [father], absolutely idolizes him. And I don't actually feel jealous of him. I'm too exhausted, I'm just delighted he's home. But as regards fathering...if he thinks something is wrong or...needs to be corrected, like he'll...lay down the law as far as he is concerned then, but he's actually quite happy to leave it up to me. But then, he comes along and does his things at the weekends...he'd never be a house-husband, but he does loads of work around the house. (Miriam, mother of William)

The father's role in doing practical and fun things, as opposed to making phone calls and complaining about services was highlighted by the mothers:

> [My husband] is great at doing practical things with him, I mean [my husband] is the one that gets him up every morning and gets him ready for school… I wasn't always here, he would do as much with him and I suppose he's, he's probably here more than me at the moment…but that I think will stop now as soon as I finish in college… I would do all of that [phone calls and letter writing] because I'd say [my husband] would never complain about anything…that's just his personality. (Margaret, mother of Jonathan)

> He's [husband] very busy at the moment, cause he has a job going out next week. When he comes in he brings them [the children] off to the park, or he brings them out to the shops, he spends more time socially with them than I do, cause I have them all day…it's different. I'm not a park person…John absolutely loves him…he keeps asking what time will Daddy be home, you know…my husband is very good with them. (Therese, mother of John)

However, despite this practical support, many mothers indicated a feeling of being given a heavier task:

> [My husband] is quiet…would sit there and he will take it all in…but I'd say he was very overwhelmed by the whole situation… Even all the ways through and still do today, I'll look up and I explain to [husband], but [husband] won't read up on this…he never does it, he never gets to it. So you feel you're carrying the whole lot. (Mary, mother of Patrick)

> I suppose at least the father is out most of the day, isn't he… I know there's big pressure on him as well, I think with the mother though, all the time, you know, you're kind of…you're there with him [the child]. (Betty, mother of Michael)

> I'd say we're together on that [child's learning disability] definitely, yeah. I'd print off stuff at work and hand it to him and say: read this, you know. But probably just that he wouldn't have the time, I think a lot of it is left to the mother, anyway, you know, but no, it was always something we could talk about, like, and we went through it together. (Laura, mother of Kevin)

> [My husband] is very good with them, yes, very, very good with them. But I think the intuition is lacking, on a normal scale, just a normal male–female scale...just that feeling something isn't right or feeling that if this goes on he's [the child] going to get hyper or whatever... I think he'd enjoy working from home, you know, he would certainly enjoy working more with the kids... He's brilliant with the kids, a great cook, but the house would be upside down and that causes stress in itself. I mean, I'm not interested in being houseproud it's just that it does help create the calmness, which we need in the house. (Margaret, mother of four)

> Everything to do with Noel, books to be read, would be me. I would go to the library, I would go to Easons and things like that, I'd say, I'd mention things out of it to [husband] and he would try to read it, but he doesn't... I think in anything to do with fathers and mothers, I think that even...when women and men go out for a drink, the woman will never relax, knowing that she's got to get up in the middle of the night and feed the child, even at this stage now, if I go out for a drink, when I come home I'll always be aware of who's getting up to go to the toilet, with [husband] it...would just pass over him and I would always maintain the reason they're like that is because they know the women will do it. (Anne, mother of Noel)

Some mothers explained that their partners could simply not, for various reasons, do the caring work that they were doing:

> I suppose, while he would back me up on everything...I would be the one doing much more of the caring and the domestics, you know, he would even go so far as to admit that he certainly wouldn't be able to do the amount of caring that I do. That he couldn't be the carer...and to cope with it and deal with it. (Mary, mother of Patrick)

> In my case, I suppose, I feel I'm the non-disabled one... If it wouldn't have been me handling it, because [my husband] wouldn't be home until eleven at night anyway... 'oh, sure, I'm a busy man and how would I have time for ringing those places?' I didn't feel bad, but I do know other families who, the father is very involved and things...[my husband] wouldn't. (Caitriona, mother of Donnacha)

> He [father of the child] can't cope with him either... He wouldn't really know, so I make all the decisions...like I have his support but...he'd

> bring him to all the hospital appointments then, because I work on those days... He'd give his opinion all right, even about the medication now, that was a very hard decision...what's the best thing for him [the child]. (Trish, mother of Robert)

Two mothers, Brenda and Mary, blamed the fathers' lack of understanding of the child's disability as the main reason why their relationship had broken up:

> He [husband] didn't want to be embarrassed and he didn't want to be bothered...he ended up screaming at them all the time and that was it... He couldn't handle them for one day, you know, like combing their hair was, you know, taking them out, you know, he could do it maybe one at a time, if he was going to the store he'd drop by and say, can I take one of them? But he couldn't do both of them. (Brenda, mother of Susan and Sally)

> He [son] went to [the special school] which was very hard for him and me, and his dad and I actually were...you know, a bit loggerheads over it. His dad was totally in disagreement with it and we actually separated around that time as well, which was doubly difficult for Donal. (Mary, mother of Donal)

The gender division in the majority of these families (13 out of 18) followed the traditional pattern of a breadwinning father and a primary caregiving mother. Most labour involving the physical care of the children and domestic work fell on the mother, and the father was usually absent a lot through work. In most cases his fathering involved more hands-on fun when he came home in the evenings or during the weekends, as pointed out by many of the mothers. Similarly, worrying about the children and searching for information are two 'mental' tasks that women appear to take on exclusively in their roles as mothers. Waltzer (1996) concludes that in the caring of babies, the socially constructed role of the mother is to 'worry'. If she does not do this, she is considered a 'bad' mother. The role of the father, then, is to tell the mother not to worry. He never feels the social pressure of worrying or looking up information on childcare, as he is not expected to do so as a father.

The added work of reading up on the child's condition and ways of helping them make progress, making phone calls, attending meetings with professionals and other tasks involved in mothering a child with special needs increases the pressure on the mother. As shown above, many of the mothers in my study tried to get the fathers to read the material that they had found helpful, but were met with resistance. One argument was that the father lacked the time, but it also appeared to be because the fathers trusted their partners to know their children's needs better than they did themselves. This argument could be supported by the fact that even in the families where the mothers were the main breadwinners, they also did the reading and the running for better services. Again, this is the 'mother worry' ascribed to the mother regardless if she is the main provider in the family or at home full time. The main impression from the narratives was that although the mother saw the father's help as invaluable, as shown in comments such as 'couldn't do it without him', there was a sense of loneliness emerging as a theme throughout the interviews. The gender division of labour was intensified and as a result the lives of the fathers and of the mothers were very different. The paradox between a 'free choice' and 'huge sacrifices' in the life of the mother can be summed up in the following extract:

> I left him [husband] pursue his career, it was a choice I made and a choice he made, we made it together with huge, huge sacrifices. I spent six months on my own at one stage, the year [daughter] was born and Eoin was only six...a week of every month he was away...huge, huge sacrifices to make up for it. I would say the amount of money we got to compensate that probably wouldn't have bought the support of having someone around, but it was a choice and I did it on purpose. We did it on purpose... The weekend we share his care. Husband would play a game of golf on a Sunday morning and I would do something different maybe on a Saturday morning. (Marie, mother of Eoin)

Marie's husband wanted to be there with her while Eoin was hospitalized for a longer period of time. But she discouraged him: 'I made him go back to work', despite admitting that she really would have loved it if he could have been around. She did it with a view to the future. She had already voluntarily sacrificed her own career and she felt that he had to remain at work in order to be able to climb the career ladder: 'Everything can't sink!' A patriarchal society, then, does not only limit the choices of the mother, but also the father. As the expectant breadwinner his opportunities to share the care for the child, should he want to do it, are restricted. He faces the risk of losing out in an increasingly competitive labour market where employees (mainly men) are expected to work more than the average 40-hour week and also embark on long business trips in order to reach the top. Whether this is a real dilemma for the men involved is not the concern of this book. It does, however, raise questions regarding what men do in their lives and how they relate to their children with special needs.

Gendered ways of thinking

All participants in this study emphasized differences between themselves and the fathers in relation to thinking about the child with special needs. This difference was evident in the form of responses to the child's diagnosis and in practical ways of dealing with the child. Three mothers of children born with Down syndrome reflected on the father's role as becoming instantly more 'public' when he had to tell people about the child's condition immediately after the birth:

> I suppose while saying that he was able to talk about it, he didn't really have a choice... He was the one that had to tell everybody because I just couldn't. You know, he had to phone around to people... He'd ring them up and say 'Had a baby boy', and they'd go 'Oh, great'...and he'd try and get the 'but' in quick before they start, you know, the congratulations, and that must have been very difficult... I suppose I was in hospital as well, whereas he was kind of out and about, he was meeting people all the time. (Margaret, mother of Jonathan)

> My husband was devastated. Well, he had a whole lot on his hands. He had to deal with me, he was phoning people telling them about Mother being dead and that we had a boy. Then he had to ring them all back again and tell them, well, family and the close friends, and let them know Andrew had Down syndrome as well. (Helen, mother of Andrew)

> He [husband] had a really hard job, I felt so sorry for him, because he's gone out and told everyone, especially at work, you know 'Got a baby boy, got a baby boy' and then he had to go back and tell everybody that he'd Down syndrome, so he was sort of out there in the firing line, if you like, whereas I was sort of...protected in the hospital. So I think he had a much harder job than I did. (Miriam, mother of William)

Miriam commented on the fact that their third child also was their first son and under 'normal' circumstances automatically would have been the heir to the family business.

> Everybody was so excited...[husband] had taken over the family business which is like everything to my father, and like The Son...there was all that kind of things to it. (Miriam, mother of William)

Betty, whose third child and only son Michael was diagnosed with Down syndrome, experienced the same feelings relating to the sex of her child:

> [T]he fact that Michael was the boy, I suppose, and the Son and the Farm thing...I think, had it, it's awful to say this, but had it been a girl wouldn't the blow have been as hard, do you know what I mean? (Betty, mother of Michael)

Although Betty nearly apologized for expressing this view, her comment reflected the reality in which families still live in Ireland. Farmers hand over their farms to their sons, sons inherit businesses from their fathers and so on. The comments made by the health nurse who later visited Betty and her husband only reinforced this gendered stereotype:

> She [liaison nurse] came from the community services...and she walked in here and she sat down at this table...and the first thing she said to [husband] was 'Are you upset that he'll never drive a tractor, he'll never work the farm for you?' (Betty, mother of Michael)

First, this nurse seemed oblivious to the fact that the couple had two daughters who could potentially inherit the farm. Second, it also disclosed a very narrow minded and pessimistic view on a disability such as Down syndrome. As far as this nurse was concerned, Michael would never be able to work on the farm. Both Betty and her husband were appalled at her statement:

> He [husband] was horrified. He couldn't believe how she came out...she didn't take up the baby, because he was in the cot, and she just said this to him [husband]... She was very stereotyped about it all and he would never go to mainstream school. (Betty, mother of Michael)

The stereotyped expectations of male and female behaviour did not only affect the fathers of children with disabilities such as Down syndrome. Marie, mother of Kevin, diagnosed with Asperger syndrome, felt that the father initially had problems relating to his son because he was not a typical 'boyish' boy who was into sports and rough games. In this case the diagnosis was a relief for both parents:

> He wouldn't be able to run fast or he's not very strong physically, he wouldn't want anyone to wrestle with him...so I mean, that's of course little boys, that's what they do, you know, they throw each other around the place... You accept it then [his difference]...this is him now, the diagnosis was a great relief to us in that we then didn't try to push him anymore to do stuff that we knew he'd never be able to do. (Marie, mother of Kevin)

Many children with Asperger syndrome and ADHD have difficulties taking part in sports activities where social interaction and team play are important factors. In many Irish families the bond between fathers and children is often built on sports-related activities (Kennedy 2002) and the lack of such a bond could affect the father negatively. Trute (1995), in exploring gender differences and psychological adjustments among Australian parents of children with disabilities, found that fathers of less disabled male children appeared to be at higher risk of depression compared to other fathers. A possible explanation to this, according to Trute, is that the father more readily accepts the child's disability if it is severe but finds it more difficult to accept it when the disability is mild and the social and economic potentials are uncertain. Another reason could be that the father finds it hard to accept that a high-functioning son just simply refuses to engage in traditional masculine sports activities, and thereby disappoints the father. The theme of fathers' relationship with their sons, however, is out of scope here but has the potential to be explored further.

Another issue that emerged in the narratives, relating to the mothers' and the fathers' different ways of thinking, was the length of time it took for mothers to notice and accept the child's disability in comparison to the father.

> I think it took a little longer, yes, at that time, I think he [husband] would certainly say 'no, once his hearing would be sorted out', I don't know was there just a slowness to accept maybe what was looking him in the face at the time, I think it was. I think he would tell you that himself, it took him slightly longer to come to terms, not in accepting it, but acknowledging it. (Mary, mother of Patrick)

> I'd say my fears to my husband, 'oh, sure he'll be alright, he'll be alright', but I think [he said so] to try and quell my fears...even now...that Patrick is diagnosed, he'd say to me 'and you were right now and you knew that all along', but behind it all I think he did know...he wanted to quell my fears, you know. (Mary, mother of Patrick)

> I would say a huge factor is that they [fathers] don't know the children like we do, because they don't spend a lot of time... In my situation my ex-husband was a, is a workaholic, so we didn't see that much of him at all...they have different expectations, I think too, of children than mothers do, for some reason... From other parents that I've spoken to, there seems to be a huge difference... They'll tell you 'He's happy, isn't he grand?', that kind of attitude from the fathers... It does cause a rift in

> between couples, hugely so that I have seen, so it almost becomes, you're fighting against the dad as well as the system...to try and get recognition. (Mary, mother of Donal)

> My husband was at a different level than I was, I had gone through a lot of this on my own because I sensed that things were wrong, he didn't sense, you know, I think mothers do...[husband] was at least 12 months behind me...so when I was coming to terms with it he was in crisis, when I had come out at the other end, he was coming to terms...and I suppose now we're on an even keel, roughly, you know. (Marie, mother of Eoin)

Paradoxically, Julie, mother of John, diagnosed with autism, found her husband's refusal to listen to the professionals' comments a great support:

> He doesn't want to know about it [autism]. He's never, ever wanted to know anything about it. [My husband] is very, very positive. Very positive. His answer to everything was 'Julie, he'll be OK, he'll be OK'. (Julie, mother of John)

Similarly, Miriam welcomed her husband's support when faced with negative comments from professionals regarding the home-based educational programme she had chosen for her son William:

> [The doctor] said we would end up mortgaging the house and being in terrible financial straits and that for a child being slightly improved and that he thought we'd be far better spending the money getting care for him here. So I thought, Oh, God...and [husband] listened to all this and he said 'Yeah, OK', he said, 'but he said he'd be slightly improved, didn't he? I mean that's coming from the professional?' I said 'Yeah'. You see, every time I'm sort of 'Oh, God, are we doing the right thing?' [my husband] is there and he's saying 'Yes', you know. (Miriam, mother of William)

The importance of having a supportive partner in dealing with professionals was emphasized by the majority of the mothers. Although the fathers had adopted a more passive role (leaving the researching/campaigning/educating tasks to the mothers), they sided with the mothers in their lonely and hard struggle for services.

> He [husband] would make, he would be very good against professionals... He would be much tougher to deal with than me... I do find myself much happier going into meeting those people with my husband by my

> side. Very often he says nothing, very often he says very little, but what he does say, you know, and I mean. Just having him there sometimes is a huge support. (Mary, mother of Patrick)

Stereotyped gender roles and differences in mothers' and fathers' ways of thinking did not generally cause any concern among the mothers. In most cases, the differences were acknowledged and explained, without any wishes for changes. Nevertheless, the two single mothers did portray their ex-partners' roles negatively and expressed a stronger sense of isolation.

> [A]nd I'm looking at this man [paediatric neurologist] and looking at [my husband] and going 'We're not doing drugs, I don't drug my children', and he [neurologist] talked right over me, like I hadn't said anything and he was looking at [my husband], like him and [my husband] are the only two talking. (Brenda, mother of Susan and Sally)

According to Brenda, her marriage broke up because of the father's inability to cope with the fact that their two girls were autistic and his way of relying on medication in order to deal with their behaviour. Brenda was totally against medication, and reacted strongly against her partner's collaboration with the professionals. All mothers acknowledged that a child with special needs challenges the relationship between couples, especially when there is a behaviour problem: 'he's able to split you as a couple' (Mary, mother of Patrick) and 'there's times [my husband] and I are at loggerheads over how to deal with Noel' (Anne, mother of Noel). However, there are conflicting data regarding the theory that having a child with a learning disability necessarily increases the divorce rate among couples (Horgan 2004).

My participants felt that existing counselling and stress management groups for parents did not benefit fathers in the same way that it had benefited the mothers. The reason behind this, according to them, was men's reluctance to open up and speak about feelings:

> I don't know would he [husband] open up as much in a group, I think he certainly would be more inclined to open up to men, you see, this little group that I'm involved in there are women and women talk and talk, there are some very good talkers in our group. I think he wouldn't find it easy, he would find it hard to get his word in sometimes. He wouldn't be pushy enough. I think he certainly would be suited to a group of four or five men. (Mary, mother of Patrick)

> [My husband] went to the first few [stress management meetings] and he came home and said 'Look, Ma, I'm not getting anything out of this'... I think it's because, like he has to deal with his feelings, you know, he had to, push him anyway to a group, like, and ask him to start on about, you know...things that are personal to him, it just doesn't work for him. I think it's a man thing. (Mary, mother of Patrick)

> He wouldn't talk about it, he hasn't told his best friends at work... He might have told one person about it... I think he feels it's private, it's personal, I don't know. (Martina, mother of Daniel)

The image of the father as a stereotyped male unable to deal with feelings emerges out of these quotes. According to the mothers, the fathers tended to keep the personal to themselves and found it difficult to talk about private matters.

Similarly, the mothers in this study were much more involved in pressure groups and campaigns:

> I suppose [my husband] has just mainly left this to me because I don't find it a problem to do it, and to go to any group to get involved, and I suppose he knew that before we got married...it just fell into place. (Mary, mother of Patrick)

> [My husband] was never able to attend the meetings, that much like, because of the fact that the girls were at school, and Michael was kind of, you know, needing a lot of attention, and he had to stay with him. So I was sort of the one who went to the meetings. (Betty, mother of Michael)

It is of importance to notice how public and private roles were reversed in some of these families. The gender divided roles of the 'public' father and the 'private' mother were in this case abandoned: the father stayed behind at home with the child and the mother was participating in decision-making and public protests. Mothers do this, I would argue, because they are empowered by their increased access to information, such as the Internet, and share this knowledge with each other at various meetings and support groups. Some mothers stated that this change in attitudes was also a reflection of a general change in society:

> I think mothers then unfortunately would not have known the way to go forwards, and never complained. They were totally dependent on the state and I just feel very sad and sorry for them because they all had to

> place their children in an institution... They didn't have the independence, they weren't able to drive, most of them wouldn't have the independence or the money or resources to cope with them. (Mary, mother of Patrick)

Mary believed that there are more choices for women now, and that they are being listened to. In this sense, equality between men and women has improved and women are being listened to more now than decades ago. I would argue, however, that there are still many mothers of children with special needs who are living under difficult financial and social circumstances in Ireland. They might not have access to the same information and education that is available for better-off mothers, such as the Internet and support groups. Women living under extremely difficult circumstances would therefore be more vulnerable and dependent on the state to take over the responsibility for their children with special needs.

Family life – a struggle

The vast majority of my participants had more than one child (in just two cases the child with special needs was the only child). The stress a child with a learning disability has on siblings and the immediate family is well documented in research (Baldwin and Carlisle 1994; Dowling and Dolan 2001; Widdows 1997). The mothers in my study confirmed these theories on the isolation of the whole family, as shown below:

> Patrick chooses to live independently of the other children in our family and for safety reasons we don't push it...so basically the other two children stuck together and made friends and just accepted it. I mean children grow up with things and are much quicker to accept it. It's a hard set-up, it's unusual that he chooses not to mix with any other in the family, but that's it... We make very conscious decisions to have family weekends when Patrick is in respite... We're like two separate families a lot of the time, we always spend Sunday apart, one has the rest of the kids and one has Patrick. (Mary, mother of Patrick)

> We don't have what you call 'a normal family' life. We can't kind of go places other families would go to, we certainly would have to think twice about them, you know. No matter where we're going or what we're doing, everything has to revolve around Jonathan... If we had another nine-year-old child in the house, like really, you wouldn't ask his siblings to baby sit, you'd just be saying 'Are you going to be home tonight

because Jonathan will be here', you wouldn't be letting him on his own as such, but they wouldn't be babysitting as such. But it's still babysitting, you're still minding a small baby. (Margaret, mother of Jonathan)

We should all be helped in the family, in our own different ways... I feel with [daughter]...I feel I sacrificed her for him. I think she is running, because I often said to her, like they'd [daughter and friends] be going to different houses now, watching videos and whatever, and I say 'why can't you come back here?', and she says 'ah, sure, but there's nothing here to do', but I think she doesn't want to bring them back here. (Mary, mother of Patrick)

[Elder brother] took it in the face time and time again...got a lot of those slaps in the back of the car now, in order to keep the two of them belted in...another thing that he lost out on big time was family journeys, you know, things that the whole family should do together, well, that's out... I think myself and [husband] decided, right, OK, John and me, we become hermits here, and that's exactly what happened. And any time we went out, it was more like field trips. A normal Sunday visit, that used to be before John was born, would be hanging around talking to my mother and father, that was gone now, because he just wrecked the place and my father couldn't, he'd never seen anything like this, sure, and I mean, they just don't understand and they, they love him I suppose, but they just couldn't understand it. (Julie, mother of John)

The best place to go with Noel is McDonald's or Burger King, but like, there's days when you'd like to go somewhere else, like going to a hotel or something, but like if Noel's dinner comes along and there's anything slightly wrong with it, he just won't eat it and he'd sit there and he'll bang the table and it'll be, you know, he can ruin it for everybody. (Anne, mother of Noel)

We've never taken him on a holiday, the other two children and my husband and myself have gone away a couple of times when Donnacha would be in respite. But I suppose I'm lucky that I was never a person who had a high social life. I like my own quiet time and I'm much happier here reading a book and let them all go...but I suppose, all the reading I had to do on it, and then I started this organization, so it must have hurt family life in some way, me going off or me on the phone trying to counsel other parents...

> When he is in respite I try and give that time to them [other children] so that means that I don't get the time, or if I'm selfish and say, look it's my day, they won't get the time. But I think they're coming of age now that they're able to, you know [son] goes down the road to his friends and plays football and [daughter] might go to her friend...but I feel guilty, you know, you're pulled both ways, because you're conscious that they need you as well. (Caitriona, mother of Donnacha)

> I feel that I neglect my daughter, because his needs are greater and I suppose everyone that has some kind of disabled child, do they feel the same? I don't know, because she's so resilient and strong, and you know, she's fine... They [daughter and son] get on great...they play...it's the best therapy you could ever have. (Marie, mother of Kevin)

There were two important themes emerging from these narratives. The first was that 'normal' family life ceased to exist in the case where the child with special needs also had behavioural problems. Outings in public, to restaurants and holidays, were risky for these families and most of them chose not to pursue them. This in turn isolated the family members and in effect disabled the whole family. Second, the mothers expressed a feeling of guilt for neglecting their non-disabled children and sacrificing their needs because of the demands of the child with a learning disability. This feeling of being torn in different directions and not having enough time certainly contributed to a feeling of stress and depression among these mothers. Paradoxically, mothers also found great comfort and support from their non-disabled children who quickly adjusted to living a family life with a difference and accepted it without any problems:

> She's [eldest daughter] much more mature than the average eight-year-old, in my mind, and would be very much a child for asking questions about Patrick and would always have been told...and I think that fact that we've been honest with her from day one has been great. (Mary, mother of Patrick)

> They [the two brothers] get on great...they always did, I mean, he'll annoy [brother] sometimes, but they wouldn't fight any more than any other two boys. I thought he'd [brother] be embarrassed first when he [Kevin] went into school and all that, he's not, you know, and some days I'd be reading the copy when [older son] would get into the car and I'd say 'Oh, Kevin had a bad day?' and he'd say 'Oh, I know, I heard him in

> the corridor' and I'll say 'Were you embarrassed about that' and 'Oh, no, my friends were saying "there's Kevin again", like, they're all very accepting of him'. (Laura, mother of Kevin)

> As far as I was concerned, I was proud of him [eldest son punched a boy in class who said his brother did not deserve to live] I thought he was great. He takes things in his stride, apart from this, it was the only time I saw him get really mad. But I think, for someone to say that your brother deserves to be dead! He obviously felt he very much deserves to be alive! (Marie, mother of Eoin)

Siblings of children with special needs learn to live a very different life in comparison to their peers who have non-disabled brothers and sisters. Nevertheless, judging by the narratives of their mothers, they get on with their own lives and they also become aware and open-minded about disabilities. When confronted with ignorance and prejudices, as in Marie's eldest son's case, they might react angrily and defensively. The ignorance in other children, I believe, has its roots in wider society where people who do not live with disabilities keep their distance because of fear of the unknown.

Avoiding the gaze of the public

While Marie's son reacted impulsively and hit back against discriminating comments regarding his brother with special needs, some mothers also felt the urge to protest loudly and clearly in public, especially when they experienced the glare of people and subsequently suspected what was on their minds:

> You keep away, because you know like, if you go into someone's house, he's going to be eyed up...you'd have no peace, you know. So you tend to stay away. You can't take him into a supermarket...and even at eight you're aware people looking at him saying 'Why don't they keep this child under control' and that's the time when I love to scream into their face 'You f***ing try and you see how smart you are!' you know what I mean. I would love to, but sure, you just bite your tongue, like, and just take him away. (Mary, mother of Patrick)

> I don't know how many times we would go into a restaurant and have all the dinner on the table and one of them would pitch a fit, it's like OK, we get up and leave. Next week we'll do it again, you know, and it didn't embarrass me, you know, if it bothers you – there's the door – you can leave the restaurant, you know. I've actually got into it with a couple of

> people, you know in restaurants, because they'd say stuff like 'Can't you make these kids behave?' or 'Can't you make those kids be quiet?' and it was like the wrong thing to say, I'll be in your face so fast and we would just leave. (Brenda, mother of Susan and Sally)

Whereas the mothers above reacted with anger to comments from the public regarding their children's behaviour, others were driven to tears. This happened, for example, to Caitriona who brought her son Donnacha to a hotel that hosted a conference on autism, where she met up with visiting experts from Canada and the US:

> We were sitting at the bar...the manager was up at the counter in the bar...Donnacha was sitting down in one of the other people's laps, I think he was the guy doing the camera work or something and he [Donnacha] kind of let a shriek and your man came over and said 'Get that child out of here if you can't keep him under control!' Now, the man...was just holding [Donnacha] while I was talking to the speech and language therapist who was over...but they were disgusted, they were shocked... I was totally gutted... All I could do was to get Donnacha and just put him into the car and drive home. But I cried all the way home, I don't even remember driving. (Caitriona, mother of Donnacha)

> You'll get dirty looks and all that...one day he touched a bag, this woman, he loves bright colours, you know, and she just had a bag, it was a plastic bag with some stuff in it obviously, and he just went over and touched it, she said 'Have you no manners on your child?' [sobbing] I said he has autism... My next door neighbour actually has a Down syndrome baby, and when he was born... We knew there was something wrong with Kevin but we didn't know what was wrong. I remember thinking, she's lucky in a way, because she knows and because when you look at him, you know he's special. (Laura, mother of Kevin)

Miriam, mother of William, born with Down syndrome, experienced the gaze of others differently:

> Ireland's kind of funny...that would fit in with how people react to, like racially, it's sort of not that dissimilar to how people might see anybody who is a little bit different...like you see, Down syndrome is very obvious, so you get people coming up...and genuinely being very sweet, and you know, they wouldn't say, hardly even look me in the eye, they certainly wouldn't even smile at me and 'Hello, how are you', you know,

> at William… We should be nice to somebody like you. (Miriam, mother of William)

I would argue that Miriam sensed a notion of 'charity' towards people who are disabled, a cultural heritage that still affects the thinking of legislators and policy makers (see Chapter 2). With this mentality people with Down syndrome, for example, will always be innocently looked upon with kindness/pity instead of recognized as individuals with the same rights as everybody else.

Keeping a distance: extended families

It was not only in the encounter with strangers in public that my participants experienced a distance. The extended family also appeared to keep a distance, according to the mothers. This distance was sometimes geographical, as the relatives such as the mother's own parents or siblings lived far away:

> We have no family around here, they're all up the country, and my parents are very old… I don't even know if they still know the word autism… I'd say they do, they do know it, they do know that he has that diagnosis, but they sort of say 'ah, he'd be grand', you know, they begin to think now that he won't be. (Laura, mother of Kevin)

In one case, the long geographical distance between the mother and her own family made her keep the child's high-functioning disability a secret from them:

> I never told my family, my own family, no. And they never even noticed, they don't see him because they live in [the north-west]. My husband's family, yes, I don't know, they don't understand it, they say that he's fine. (Marie, mother of Kevin)

One family decided to move abroad for a while, as a way of getting away from the extended family, which they felt was unsupportive and added to the stress:

> We moved to France, it was part of my husband's work. We were just glad to put all the past behind us, and we just felt if we were under less stress from family and friends, you know, relatives and doctors and maybe if we could get a grip on John's behaviour ourselves, because at this stage his behaviour was just terrible, terrible… I have no one left really [extended family] but my husband's family, they just don't understand…they don't

> want to know, it's all, you know, we're not strict enough. (Margaret, mother of four children with special needs)

One mother, Trish, experienced pressure from her immediate family, including her own mother, to send the child away when he showed signs of being a child with special needs:

> She [mother] thought I should put him into [service provider] or somewhere, they [family] thought 'just get rid of him'...they were just totally allergic to him...my mother's answer to the problem was 'get rid of him'. (Trish, mother of Robert)

Margaret, whose mother was of a great help to her, nevertheless encountered the same attitude of 'getting rid of him' from an old aunt:

> I suppose my family...my mother was great now at the time, I mean, she's been ill since now and she's just not able for him, he's too active. But she was very good at the time, now I have to say. A lot of the family, well some, not a lot, I think they were half afraid, certainly they wouldn't have been as obliging about babysitting as they would have for any other child.
>
> I remember an aunt of mine...saying to me we should put him into, she mentioned the name of a home, and she said 'if you put him in there, you know, they'll do great things with him'...they'll do great things with him... I never talked to her about it because I wasn't that close to her anyway, you know, but she can't look at him, if I happen to have him with me and I meet her, she can't look at him. (Margaret, mother of Jonathan)

Betty and Anne, on the other hand, felt that their extended families were too occupied with their own business and never initiated practical help and support:

> The [extended] families are OK, really, but I feel they're all working and I feel there's no one really who'd pick up the phone to say, look, I'll take him today for you. (Betty, mother of Michael)
>
> I've got only one sister and [husband] has seven brothers and sisters... and although they're all scattered and all that I never got any help from anybody, there was nobody ever offered me any, my own sister would have been there, and she would take my kids, at some stage she would

> take them, you know, but never, I mean we'd never really get away for a weekend of anything like that. (Anne, mother of Noel)

Many of my participants expressed dissatisfaction with the support and help from the extended family. One positive exception was generally made regarding the support of the mother's own mother, who in many cases provided both practical and emotional support. In one exceptional case, the father-in-law who lived with the family provided invaluable support in helping out minding the siblings. Informal respite, where family and friends share the care, is reported to be the most preferable type of respite (Sharpley, Bitsika and Efremidis 1997; Stalker and Robinson 1994; Trute 1995) by parents of children with special needs. Their stress level is greatly reduced if they can rely on their own family members for help. Unfortunately, few of the mothers in this book had this informal support from their extended families. One contributing factor to this was geographical: the family living with the child with special needs lived far away from their parents and extended families. Furthermore, recent changes in the labour market with both partners working reduce the availability of informal help from the wider family. This could include the mothers whose own mothers are outside the home working during the day and therefore are unavailable to share the care of the child. Other reasons for the lack of support from the extended families, as pointed out by the mothers, included the age of grandparents and their general lack of understanding of disabilities such as autism. These views reflected a closed society where children with disabilities used to be put away. My participants had no intentions of hiding their children from the rest of society because of their differences, but many of them felt pressurized to convince others that they were indeed 'good' mothers.

The notion of the 'good' mother

Anne, mother of Noel, diagnosed with ADHD/Asperger syndrome, wished that she could explain to other people about her son's behaviour:

> I would love to stand up in the school and say 'My name is Anne O'Connor and my son is Noel O'Connor and I'd like to explain to you what it [Asperger syndrome] is and apologize to you for whatever my son has done to your son. (Anne, mother of Noel)

The mother's feeling of guilt and her need to defend herself and her child, such as in Anne's case, is a product of the social construction of motherhood.

Mothers whose children do not fit in have failed in their 'jobs' as mothers and they struggle hard to avoid this perceived failure. Feminist writers on motherhood have analysed society's labelling of 'good' versus 'bad' mothers (Croghan and Miell 1998; Ladd-Taylor and Ulmansky 1998; Malacrida 2003). The patriarchal definition of motherhood (Rich 1977) prescribes the criteria for 'good' mothering, whereas 'bad' mothers are considered to be the opposite: unmarried, single, too young or too old, homosexual, living in poverty or working full time. Mothers of children with special needs also experience an added stigma attached to their capacity of mothering. This is particularly true for mothers of children with autism (Gray 1993; McDonnell 1993) where anti-social behaviour counteracts the mother's attempts to present the child favourably in public environments.

Some mothers in my research showed an increased defiance and resilience against the assumptions of 'bad' mothering. For instance, Julie, mother of John, diagnosed with autism, had a message for the general public which sums up what all mothers in my research want the public to think about if they encounter a child behaving oddly: 'Don't stare! Just do not do that.' Many mothers agreed with her:

> I would ask people to be aware of what this is, what ADHD and Asperger's is, I mean that not every child you see being bold is necessary bold, and you know, you'd ask people don't condemn these children, don't pass comment on them. (Anne, mother of Noel)

> A message to people in general: Be kinder! Make a bit of an effort! These children are just not bold, odd or weird. You have to have considerations for all kinds of people across the board. While I'm shopping Daniel might do something odd, he might flap his hands, speak very loudly in an American accent or swing between the counters at the check out desks in the shop, but I just keep going, I don't want to explain to people. (Martina, mother of Daniel)

Jumping to conclusions and passing judgements on mothers can have devastating effects and contribute to isolate and marginalize this group of women even further. Some of the mothers in this research experienced feelings of guilt, sorrow and anger at the lack of understanding from the public.

Paradoxically, the constant worry and guilt over not being a 'good mother' was sometimes exacerbated within settings such as parents' support groups:

> I had somebody at a meeting last week talking about their child with Down syndrome going to university and getting a degree. And you see, now whether I'm selling my child short, or whether I'm being realistic, I don't know, but with the best will in the world, I can never see Jonathan doing that, you know. Maybe her child will. Who am I to say? And then I sit back then when I come home and I think about it and I think, you know, is she doing something that I should be doing, should I be doing more with him, should I be pushing him more? I think, God, is she a better mother than me, because God, her child is going to get a degree, like, and my child, if he can struggle through until he's 18 and get a job stacking shelves in the supermarket and I think he'll have achieved loads. (Margaret, mother of Jonathan)

Margaret's guilt over not 'doing more with him', I would argue, is a feeling probably shared by many mothers of children with learning disabilities. This is particularly true in the era of the Internet, where numerous websites provide information on various different teaching methods and promise to improve your child's development. For a mother working full time outside the home, as in Margaret's situation, it is very difficult to keep up to date with all information, never mind spending time working with the child. Margaret relied on the Internet for some information, 'I think I'm fairly up to what he's entitled to', but trusted his special school to take care of his educational needs. It was this decision that caused the dilemma for Margaret: Was she really doing everything she could for him as his mother? This maternal conflict between caring responsibilities and other life projects has also been highlighted in a Cross-Nordic study (Hautamäki 1997). One way of alleviating strain for mothers of children with disabilities, according to Hautamäki, is to find 'the optimal balance between their needs and the needs of the child' (p.48).

Another mother, Marie, felt that if she showed signs of needing too much help from the service providers, she would be considered a 'failure' as a mother:

> I thought, I'm strong, I'll manage, I didn't want to look like some 'God help us', that can't pull her life together. Even though I do firmly believe in looking for what you are entitled to, I thought by overly doing it that I was sort of showing up that I was a failure. So you were caught between the devil and a deep blue sea. (Marie, mother of Eoin)

Similarly, Croghan and Miell's (1998) research on British clients of welfare agencies discusses how mothers employ strategies of resistance against professionals when faced with accusations of not being able to cope. The mothers in this study experienced a social stigma of being 'bad mothers' at risk of losing custody over their children. Although my participants were from much more secure financial and social circumstances, the expectations regarding women's responsibilities as mothers still had a negative effect on them. In their capacity as mothers of children with special needs, their self-esteem and identity were under constant threat from the professionals. One way to cope with this dilemma is to be resistant (Malacrida 2003) or to convince professionals that in spite of the difficulties, the mother, like any 'ordinary' mother, is doing the best she can for her child (Todd and Jones 2003).

Another dilemma causing guilty feelings among the mothers was the question whether or not to medicate the child. Four of my participants had made decisions to give Ritalin to their children in order to improve their behaviour.

> They [multi-disciplinary team] kind of told us we could decide to put him on medication. We asked, they gave us all leaflets to read about the medication, and we read it, and we kind of got stuff from the Internet and we got books, and we read up on it to see the pros and cons of this medication. So we decided to put him on the Ritalin, and he started off on a very small dose. (Anne, mother of Noel)

Anne and her husband have kept Noel on the medication ever since because they believed that it did something for him and it kept him out of trouble. The school also saw a huge difference in him as he started the Ritalin.

> I mean, with Noel you could, in the mornings, he's so hyper and he's making all sorts of weird sounds, and banging, you know and stamping around the place, and you can't get him dressed or anything like that, but when you've given him his Ritalin, like you could time it, to about 20 minutes and suddenly he becomes this most angelic child that you can talk to. (Anne, mother of Noel)

Mary, mother of Patrick diagnosed ADHD, remembered the difficulties in deciding whether or not to try Ritalin:

> [T]hey [multi-disciplinary team] recommended the Ritalin and we went away and we talked about it and whatever and we sat down and there was many flipping times like of being upset about it and wondering like were you putting your child on this like and then the side effects of it and are you gonna damage him and all this, like. (Mary, mother of Patrick)

It was when things deteriorated in school that Mary and her husband decided to go ahead with the medication, and the effect was immediate:

> We were watching him and I kept him out of school for a week to see how he'd get on...and he seemed to be, he was fine on it, you know, and once we kind of got over the fear of giving it to him...like he got on fine. (Mary, mother of Patrick)

Although Patrick's school situation improved immensely with the Ritalin, Mary felt that both his appetite and his sleep patterns were affected negatively. She also became worried about his lack of interest in socializing with others:

> My major concern about him was that even though school was very good, in the Ritalin status then, he wouldn't go outside the door. He would stay at home on his own. He wanted to see nobody, he was quite happy in his own company, you know, he would sit there, he would go upstairs and play the play station, or he'd, you know, he didn't want to see anybody, he didn't want go outside the door, which at the time was very upsetting to us, why doesn't he want to go out...You know, when you see him sitting there like, and you, he didn't want to do anything or go anywhere, you know, but I would say that would have been the Ritalin again, calming him down. (Mary, mother of Patrick)

Patrick stayed on Ritalin for two years and his school reports were full of praise during this time. Paradoxically, the school was refused a resource teacher because it was felt that Patrick managed very well without one. This particular case could be used as an argument by parents and professionals who feel that children are medicated in order to fit into the system instead of being given appropriate support in the schools. Mary, however, felt that the Ritalin helped Patrick cope with school, although she was sad to see that it 'dulled his spirit to a certain extent'. At the time of the first interview, Patrick had been taken off Ritalin due to developing severe tics and Mary reported that he was once again 'in trouble' in school.

Margaret, mother of Jonathan born with Down syndrome, went privately to a paediatrician who diagnosed Jonathan as hyperactive and prescribed Ritalin. Margaret felt that Jonathan did function better while on Ritalin, but resented the fact that she had to go private in order to get somebody to monitor his medication. Another mother, Trish, had a negative experience of using Ritalin on her son Robert, whose behaviour deteriorated drastically after being given the medicine. During the years professionals had tried him on various anti-depressants and at the follow-up meeting Trish felt that he at long last was on a combination of drugs that seemed to work. Robert's current medication had been prescribed by a consultant based in London as the local psychiatrist had no experience of prescribing that particular drug.

Mary, mother of Patrick, autistic and severely learning disabled, also had a long history of trying different medications in order to prevent her son from self-injuries and extremely challenging behaviour. Although Mary depended on the expertise from the psychiatrists that she dealt with, she wanted to have some form of control over what kind of drugs were used:

> He was put on Valium at four, which I didn't agree with, but the doctor that was working with [service provider] at the time strongly advised it. And I made it clear to her that I never agreed with it. I agreed to do it for a short period and very limited time. I was never happy with Valium. (Mary, mother of Patrick)

The prescription of Valium for a four-year-old child is, I would hope, an exception rather than a rule as far as helping families living with autism. It does, however, reflect a society still relying heavily on old forms of medication, instead of developing proper provisions for children and adolescents in need of psychiatric care.

Catholic values and children with special needs

Many of the mothers had experienced comments from people reflecting old religious beliefs such as the child with special needs being 'a special gift from God' or 'a cross that has to be carried'. In all cases except one, these comments evoked anger among the mothers.

> That's a lot of rubbish, I'd get quite a lot of that...utterly rubbish! Especially, I suppose, mostly among the old generation. And you'd be surprised in the attitudes of some of the younger mothers...you know, and I hate the pity...you know, the pity when you see people's faces. I hate that. I hate Patrick being pitied. And I do get quite a lot of them [looks] and I do hate that attitude of, you know, 'you were chosen to rear this child!' and this and that... Only people that are not in that position [are] saying that. They wouldn't say that to other parents, to me that's more ignorance and choosing to keep their heads in the clouds, really. (Margaret, mother of Patrick)

Crap. Crap...oh, people say that, yeah, yeah, but it's always people that don't know what they're talking about. (Margaret, mother of Jonathan)

Oh, yeah, well, I would say I've got that from the family [laugh]...the older generation now...got it a bit in mainstream school when he was younger, all right, from a teacher. (Mary, mother of Donal)

I think that's [a cross to carry] a lie from the pit. Within the Catholic Church, and very much in Irish tradition, a child with special needs would be a curse, you had done something wrong, and now you were paying for it, or somebody in your family has. I think it is a lie from the pit and I totally reject it. (Helen, mother of Andrew)

I used to get very annoyed when people used to tell me about the special parents and these special children were sent to these special parents, that used to...that still irritates me now. And if you weren't able to bear this cross, you wouldn't be sent a cross. I thought that was a great load of bullshit, and I thought, spare me. I just wouldn't listen to it, you know... It'd be people passing, maybe older people, or not necessarily like, I mean a couple of nurses in the hospital said it to me, like. (Betty, mother of Michael)

That's [cross or a special gift] an awful lot of rubbish... I'm a practising Catholic because that's the way I was brought up and [husband] was brought up that way as well, which is grand. I see it very much as a kind of, as a club kind of that you're part of and it brings you into the community and it's important the boys get to know...as regards a relationship with God and God saying 'right, she has strong, strong shoulders, and we'll send her down...', that's a lot of rubbish...people say to me 'oh, he gave that burden to you cause he knew you were able, and sure, you're special', you're no more special than anyone else! You know, they'll throw it and it won't do you a lot good at that time, you know. (Julie, mother of John)

I've come across it, yeah, yeah...crap...[laugh]. I don't know am I a better person because of him, I don't think I'm a great saint. Because I look after him I feel very well, but there are moments, huge moments where I feel resentful, bitter, sad, lonely, on my own, no one understands. So how could I feel I'm this saint? How could I feel, no, I don't feel God gave him to me, I do however, I'm a realist, and I do believe he's here, he's mine. I'm his mother, it's my duty to look after him, to care for him and to

> love him, and that's how I look at it and over my dead body [laugh] will I not do those things...whether or not God has anything to do with it...I very much doubt it...people who know me and who know the situation, even if they were religious...because they see exactly what I go through, and they see him being sick and they see, they wouldn't dream of saying sort of 'oh, sure he's a gift from God', because they just know too much. People who can't cope with the world say that, people who can't cope with reality. They're doing it to cheer themselves up, because if they knew me, it doesn't cheer me up. Like if God chose me, he needn't have bothered, you know. (Marie, mother of Eoin)

> I've heard that being said [a special gift from God] nobody said it to me, thank God, because I would be, I would think that's an insult to Daniel, I would think that is a terrible thing to say, he's him and he's a great person and you know, I hate that attitude. (Martina, mother of Daniel)

> Yeah, yeah, a load of woolly! [laugh] That's all I can say, but again, it's the Irish way to deal with a hurtful situation. But trying to tell you that it's, that you're lucky nearly, it's a load of...it's the Irish way of doing it and it's all, if they could only see themselves, that's the way. (Caitriona, mother of Donnacha)

As shown above, the mothers confirmed that religious statements such as 'a gift from God' or 'a cross' were frequently made by people in the context of the child with a learning disability. The participants stressed that these remarks would be made by people who do not understand the situation and who would make them in order to comfort themselves more than the mothers. The dismissive remarks were often followed by a laugh from the mother, to underline how far removed such a person would be from reality. As far as the mothers were concerned, comments like these were anything but helpful and they inflicted more hurt through revealing an underlying ignorance regarding children with special needs.

Landsman (1999) discusses the concept of a child with special needs as a 'special gift from God' in her ethnographic study on American mothers. Her narrators reject this statement for several reasons: first because it diminishes the child's personhood (it has less value than a non-disabled child), second because of the 'romantic glossing over of the pain and hardship involved' (p.144) in mothering a child with special needs and third because of 'the notion that prior to the child's birth they were somehow very different from normal people' (p.144). The gift rhetoric is not totally rejected, however, but the mothers use it to describe what their special children have given them. It is the child not God that brings a gift of unconditional love to the mother. I agree with this redefinition in which, according to Landsman, mothers of children with disabilities reassess their values, put things in perspective. Furthermore, this gift-rhetoric, I would argue, does not patronize the mother to feel obliged to care for a 'gift from God' in silence. Instead it acknowledges that a child with special needs can bring about positive changes in the mother's life, such as a different perspective on life and an increased awareness regarding the norms of personhood in society. One of my participants strongly agreed with this:

> It is true, I mean, he has given me a lot. I wouldn't have the interest and the passion for learning, you know, and there's a whole future ahead of me, where there wouldn't have been, which sounds awfully selfish, but there is because of him, and he has sparked that interest, which is great. (Martina, mother of Daniel)

It is of interest to notice that some of the participants found the religious comments typically 'Irish', an Irish way of dealing with something uncomfortable. As a contrast, the only mother who had felt comfort in hearing the words 'special gift' was the American mother whose Irish roots brought her back to live here:

> I thought I wasn't supposed to have children, and I went against God and had them with science, you know, so I went through a horrible guilt that this is my fault. And then my uncle came up from Florida, he drove all the way up to tell me this, and he says 'It's your perspective, you're looking at it wrong', he said, 'you have to understand, God gives these children to special people, he gave you two.' It was like an honour to be trusted with these children, because they are special, you know...oh, yeah, it opened my eyes what I had been entrusted with two very special souls, and if God didn't think I could do it, I wouldn't have gotten them, you know, so yeah...it was like, OK, if God trusted me with these children, then I will do my very best, you know. (Brenda, mother of Susan and Sally)

Brenda's reaction to her uncle's comforting words was in sharp contrast to the Irish mothers' views on the same statement. For them the remark was evidence of an ignorant and conservative society where mothers are provided with no help or understanding in their efforts to bring up a child with special needs. For Brenda it was a turning point and gave her the strength to keep going. I believe that the two very different reactions reflect the cultural context in which the mothers lived. The Irish mothers were critical of the Catholic Church and therefore dismissed remarks associated with that religious tradition. Brenda, on the other hand, had grown up in a family that glorified Ireland and its culture and thus associated her uncle's words with hope.

The dismissal of the 'gift of God' theme by mothers of children with disabilities has, according to other mothers, resulted in an extreme image of struggle by 'activist-mothers' (Horgan 2004, p.197). One of the research participants in Horgan's study wanted to see a happy medium between the image of the hard struggle for services and the image of the gift from God. However, as Horgan points out, the image of the eternal struggle sadly reflects the reality for mothers and they are therefore likely to continue to voice their dissatisfaction. It is also important to notice that although my research participants rejected being called 'special' and 'chosen by God' many of them would still consider themselves practising Catholics who regularly go to Mass. Some of the mothers said that their faith was weaker now in comparison to before they had a child with special needs. Paradoxically, others would argue that only through a faith in God had they been able to cope.

> Having Patrick would have weakened my religion...yes, it would have. It would have weakened my belief. Because, I suppose, I lost a brother...through tragic circumstances...my faith helped me through that, it certainly brought my mother through it and it would have brought me through it. I must admit that having suffered the death of two parents and having suffered two miscarriages... Patrick was put there again to challenge me and I felt, yes, that sometimes it could be the last straw that would break the camel's back. It was too much of a challenge, almost at times, you know, so I must say that weakened my faith quite a bit... I think basically the fact that I have other children, and a child approaching communion, keeps me going. For my child's sake, you know, and as a family. But me personally, I wouldn't have had as strong a faith as I did 10–15 years ago. (Mary, mother of Patrick)

> We are Catholics, yeah... I suppose like, I pray a lot now. I did lose faith for a while, I suppose...I still feel like there'd be something, some greater power there, somewhere. At times I got very disillusioned, though. (Betty, mother of Michael)

> We are practising Catholics without a big hang up about it [laugh] you know... I think that in our family, we go to Mass every Sunday because I think I do believe in that and I do believe in the strength you get from

> receiving that gift, and I do believe I'm going to a flawed church, flawed people, but at the end of the day, I just take the flaws, I don't condone them. (Margaret, mother of four children with special needs)

> I would have been brought up as a Catholic and not an overly religious person, I would have time to talk to God when I had time, I reckon he understood... My husband would be a lot more bitter, he doesn't go to Mass and he feels very let down and all that kind of thing. But when I go into the respite centre and I see all the other little kids there, in a wheelchair and they're in a corner, and you come back in an hour's time and they're still in a corner whereas Donnacha has been a little boy, now he may always be a little boy when he's 60, but he's doing everything a little boy should do, so I have no reason to be...you know, mad with God. (Caitriona, mother of Donnacha)

Three mothers declared that they were 'not religious at all'. These mothers were the youngest participants (early and mid 30s) in the study and living in urban areas. Their attitudes reflected the current changing trend in Irish society where more and more people indicate that they have no religion (Central Statistics Office 2004b).

> No, I'm not into religion [laugh] I wouldn't even think why? You know, that's life and everybody's life is different. (Laura, mother of Kevin)

> I'm not religious at all, I mean...Daniel is making his first communion, but only because it's expected from grandparents, and I don't really bring them [the children] to Mass and stuff, I just don't. (Martina, mother of Daniel)

> No, I wouldn't be a bit religious, I wouldn't be praying for him... My friend's mother, she was always praying for him [laugh] I wouldn't be praying for him, sure if he's that way, what's there to pray for? No, I just say he's there and that's the way he is...you can't change it. (Trish, mother of Robert)

One of the eighteen mothers had left the Catholic Church at a young age and become a Born Again Christian. She found enormous strength in her faith:

> I believe whatever happens to me, God has ordained it. Or God knows all about it. The way I would view it is that all my children are gifts from God. So when we discovered we were expecting Andrew and he wasn't planned, we knew that God overruled our plans. God had another plan in

> place. I would feel as a mother, that there are demands put upon you that bring out things in your character that are latent to that point. And you find grace in situations, the grace of God. (Helen, mother of Andrew)

The choices of having more children: amniocentesis and abortion

Some of the mothers acknowledged that the birth of their child with special needs made them reflect on child bearing in a different way than they would have had if the same child had been born non-disabled. In one case this took the form of genetic counselling before the next child was conceived. Another young mother decided that in order to cope with her child with ADHD she could not have any more children.

> We had genetic counselling...we were interested in having another baby and we were told, no, it won't repeat itself. He [doctor] thought it just shouldn't stop you having other kids, and neither should it stop you living a life, you could just totally get absorbed in Eoin and not live a life. (Marie, mother of Eoin)

> It changed... Definitely I didn't want any more children...like I knew when he was two that I definitely didn't want any more and I was only 21 myself then. (Trish, mother of Robert)

The difference in the two quotes above could be explained by the different circumstances in which these two mothers were living. Marie was married and financially well off whereas Trish, at the age of 19, had faced an unplanned pregnancy and raised her boy, who had severe behaviour problems, as a single mother. Although Trish had reunited with her son's father and was engaged a year after the initial interview and Robert's behaviour had improved immensely, she still maintained her decision of not having any more children: 'I've no patience then with everybody else's children, because I kind of have to keep it all for him... I feel like I have enough to cope with...' (Trish, mother of Robert). When asked about amniocentesis and abortion, Trish expressed a liberal view as far as other women were concerned: 'They should have a choice.' However, when faced with the hypothetical question regarding her own son, she immediately said no: 'He's here now and you just have to live with it...it's not that bad.' Marie, another mother of a boy diagnosed ADHD, spoke about her feeling of guilt when she sometimes wished he had never been born.

> It's a terrible thing to say and it's an awful thing, like as regards the mother...I mean this is an alien thing to a mother to say like that...because some days you say, Jesus like, what did I do wrong? Am I so bad? You know, for this to be landed on me. (Mary, mother of Patrick)

The image of the 'good' mother was yet again inflicting guilt on these mothers, who had the courage to admit that they sometimes wished that the child with special needs did not exist. This feeling, I would argue, is probably much more common than we know, but it is something that is hardly ever mentioned, as it is 'an alien thing for a mother to say'. One mother in this study spoke about how she felt lonely and unsupported amongst other parents when sharing her honest views:

> I'd say my first Down syndrome meeting...everybody there was kind of, you know, they'd be talking to you and saying, you know, 'I wouldn't change my child for the world'; 'I never wished that they were normal or whatever.' I still wish he was born normal. I still wish he was born without Down syndrome. But I think if he was born with something else, I would also wish he didn't have it, if it was just something physical. I mean, why would you, why would you ask for your child to have something wrong with him? And I would certainly be an exception there, and people think when you say that, that you're rejecting your child. I don't reject him... But the reality is that he has Down syndrome and we really, when I got pregnant, we weren't all saying 'Oh, God, we wish we have a child with Down syndrome,' we were all saying 'God, I hope this child is going to be a normal, healthy, happy child.' (Margaret, mother of Jonathan)

Margaret's objection was not against her child per se, but to the taboo on speaking honestly about what it feels like to have a child born with special needs.

Disability researchers contribute to this taboo by arguing that by allowing these negative voices to be heard is in fact discriminating against people with disabilities (McLaughlin 2003). Thus, researchers are discouraged to unearth voices depicting a life full of hardship and struggle in the context of a child born with, for example, Down syndrome. Instead they advocate research approaches that would deter women from choosing an abortion when learning that their unborn child has a disability. This strategy does very little to empower and support mothers of children with disabilities who have the right to be heard regardless of what their honest feelings are. Miller and Rock

(1998) argue that aborting a disabled unborn child is not so much the wish of the mother, but rather the wish of a society that discriminates against disabilities. This would also be the view of anthropologist Rapp (1995) who discusses the pros and cons of amniocentesis. Rapp argues that the medical profession can do very little to alleviate risks for expecting mothers, and that the real risks for unborn children can be found elsewhere: poverty, crime, drug abuse, lack of education and appropriate health services. This is, in my opinion, very true and it is an issue that certainly should be addressed. Nevertheless, who has the right to judge a woman whose choice is to abort her unborn child with a disability? In this perfect world, where women have so many choices, those who are well off might opt for cosmetic surgery to take care of excessive fat and wrinkles. Perhaps genetic counselling and amniocentesis will be the future 'cosmetic surgery' to remove unwanted disabled children from our world? On the other hand, is it right to say that these children are unconditionally welcomed by their mothers, and that it is only society that discriminates against them? Are we to condemn mothers who choose to abort a child whom they know will be severely disabled? These issues are very important in the discussion on motherhood and need to be addressed with more vigour.

Questions regarding amniocentesis and abortion in the context of autism and ADHD are purely hypothetical, as these disabilities cannot be detected during pregnancy. Furthermore, in the Irish context, even if, for example, Down syndrome could be detected, a decision to terminate such a pregnancy would cause extra difficulties for the mother who then would have to travel abroad for an abortion. None of my participants with children with Down syndrome or severe learning disabilities would have opted for an abortion had they known about their child's disability. Many of them, however, expressed their support for other women who, in similar circumstances, might decide to terminate their pregnancies.

> Yes, I think they [women expecting children with severe disabilities] should have the right to choose that. I don't know what I would have done, to be honest with you, I think that would have been a decision between the two of us. I really couldn't tell you. I didn't have the amniocentesis, but if it had come about somehow, or if it had been discovered, I really don't know what we would do. That worries me, but I don't know. But I'd like to think that because I made the decision to have her [fourth child] that I would have gone through with it. I don't know, I really don't.

> But I certainly feel that people should have a choice. (Mary, mother of Patrick)

> I often thought of that [amniocentesis] I often felt like – what if I had known then? Because I often think that there's a fate worse than death as well, do you know what I mean? But I still probably would feel, yes, I would go ahead and carry him, you know, I wouldn't have had an abortion at the time... I think they [other women] should have a choice, yeah, I think they should...it's a long, hard road. (Betty, mother of Michael)

Paradoxically, Betty was one of four mothers in my study who expressed a wish for more children, despite the challenges of living with a child with special needs.

> Down in the back of my mind, I wanted to have another baby, I kept thinking, well if Michael had some little companion with him, that he would be a help with...that the two of them would be together and be company sort of for each other...it was for him I was thinking of it, really. So anyway, I was pregnant, and you know, to say it was a planned pregnancy again, with the result that everything ended in disaster for the second time around. (Betty, mother of Michael)

Due to medical circumstances, Betty lost her baby and ended up having a hysterectomy later. She suffered physically during the months of this second pregnancy during which time her son's heart surgery also took place. Her mental wellbeing was also challenged by professionals who did not support her wish for more children.

> The social worker, the lady that came out, didn't encourage it at all. And there was no encouragement from the paediatrician or from anybody, that they felt maybe at 37 I shouldn't have any more children, but I still didn't think I was old...more or less I was told...I shouldn't be thinking of any more children. (Betty, mother of Michael)

Mary, whose eldest son Patrick had autism and a severe learning disability, had problems convincing her husband about having a fourth child:

> No, he wasn't at all impressed [laugh] with my convictions, he felt we had two other healthy children and we had enough of a challenge and I think he worried a great deal how it was going to affect me. I thought about genetic counselling, somebody else had told me about that, and I opted

> not to go for it...in the end of the day you get all the advice and you get it all in front of you, but of course you have to make the decision. So I felt there was no point going down that road... I wanted this baby. I wondered at times was I absolutely mad, but more often than not I knew I was right. I don't know why, it was just a very, very strong feeling. A gut feeling. I took a risk... I didn't want to use Patrick as an excuse not to have her [fourth child] because I felt and I knew I would in a couple of years time turned back and said, well, I would have had another baby only for Patrick, and I felt it wasn't fair to land something on Patrick... I was worried I'd end up resenting Patrick to a certain extent because of that. (Mary, mother of Patrick)

Both Betty and Mary went ahead with their pregnancies despite being discouraged by people around them. In Betty's case the lack of support from professionals and their attitudes of her being 'too old' added to her misery, especially when this pregnancy terminated due to medical reasons. Instead of listening to Betty and understanding her reasons for wanting another child, the medical professionals defended a socially constructed model of motherhood and passed judgements on how and when mothers should have children. In Betty's case, both the health nurse and the paediatrician appeared to be of the view that a mother who already has a child with special needs, and is in need of support services, acts irresponsibly and irrationally if she decides to have more children. Thus her own arguments are dismissed and her reproductive choices limited. In Mary's case, her husband worried about how she would cope with the pressure of having another baby, knowing that the services were so thin on the ground. Mary, however, was determined not to let her child's special needs affect her personal choice in a negative way, and still felt entitled to support from the service provider. It was in fact the birth of Mary's fourth child that made her determined to fight for shared care for her son Patrick.

> It just really dawned on me, even though I knew it all at the time, that there was an awful lot depending on me. So that if I go down, or if anything happened to me, [husband] would have three other children to cope with...and I just knew that some things had to be put in place here. I just decided, right, I want a decent system in operation if, God forbid, anything happened to me, number one, because I am his number one carer. (Mary, mother of Patrick)

A year after the initial interview, Mary had fought long and hard to get more respite care for Patrick. With the help of a solicitor's letter she had achieved respite every second weekend compared to the previous respite of two days every second month. The ultimate aim of shared care – where Patrick would spend half of the time at home and half of the time in care had not materialized yet, as the service provider did not offer such a service. Yet, Mary showed resilience and determination as she decided to follow her urges and have another child.

Miriam, mother of William, with Down syndrome, felt that, in hindsight, a larger family would have benefited both her and William. Instead of living in a nuclear family, she saw an alternative:

> I think it would have been really nice to be in that kind of an old-fashioned family set up, you know, where...in a big house with lots of people... I often think that we're lucky that...that we don't have to hide our child at home in the kitchen, that they can actually be part of the family... I think I would have, in hindsight, had more children after him. A bigger family, so that he would have had siblings around his age. I think that would have been good. (Miriam, mother of William)

Conclusion

The narratives confirm a traditional and strong gender divide within the families where the mothers took on the traditional role of childcare and housework. Many of them stressed that this was done as a matter of choice. This maternal work (as discussed throughout the book) involved running for services, searching for information and reading literature relevant to the child's disability. It is very important to note that, according to the mothers, none of the 18 fathers were involved in this agency for their children. This included the two families where the mothers were in fact the main breadwinners and the father was a casual, part-time worker. In most cases, the mothers passed on literature and information to their partners who sometimes did read it, and other times declined to do so. Fathers' reasons for not reading the material, according to the mothers, was their lack of time or them trusting the mothers to know best. Despite this passive role in the family, the fathers' support and input was rated as equally important to that of the mothers and many of the participants stressed that they could not do without them. The fathers' tasks were more of a practical, hands-on nature, having fun with the children after work and taking them to parks and playgrounds. Some fathers also took the children to various therapies and appointments after the day's work 'and never did I hear the man complain' (Julie) or accompanied the mothers to meetings with professionals. This moral and psychological support from the father was highly appreciated and many participants were satisfied with this division of labour.

There was, however, sometimes both a subtle and an overt dissatisfaction with the father's lack of involvement in the care of the child. Some mothers expressed a feeling of loneliness in dealing with the child with special needs: 'you're carrying the whole lot' (Mary) and 'a lot of it is left to the mother' (Laura). Two single mothers reported that the fathers' lack of understanding of the child's special needs eventually led to a marital breakdown. As already mentioned, the majority of the mothers appeared to be satisfied with their marriages and able to solve problems together with their partners. The reason behind this, I would argue, was that many of the mothers were at home full time, or worked part time, and thereby had the time and energy to invest in dealing with matters relating to the child. This situation will probably change as more and more women move into the labour market. The mundane tasks of caring for a child with a disability combined with fighting/campaigning for services will take a heavier toll on a mother who also has to work outside the home, unless the father shares the traditional mothering duties with her.

The possibility of the father sharing the maternal work, however, appeared slim, judging by the narratives of the mothers: 'the maternal thinking is different...it's needed...it does help create the calmness' (Margaret). Other mothers reported that their husbands could never be 'a carer' (Mary) or 'house husband' (Miriam) and do the work that they did. Without going deeper into the debate as to whether or not there are biological differences between mothers and fathers in parenting a child, I argue that the social expectations of mothers and fathers do shape our thinking. This was also evident amongst the mothers: the expectations of a male 'heir' to the family business ended up in disappointment (not necessarily for the fathers but for people in their surroundings) and the sport-interested father found it hard to accept that his only son disliked rough and tumble games. Another theme explored in this chapter was family life. The mothers revealed how difficult it was to live a 'normal' family life when one child has special needs, in particular when the child has behaviour problems. They were reluctant to visit people and go to public places such as restaurants. Their choices of leisure activities and holidays for the whole family were also very limited. The siblings of the child with special needs had to make many sacrifices, according to many of the mothers, who also expressed a constant feeling of guilt for neglecting their non-disabled children. There were, however, also positive effects reported by the mothers regarding the siblings' ways of dealing with learning disabilities. They became more broadminded and accepting of differences in society in general and thus were a great support to the mothers themselves.

The mothers also experienced a huge amount of negative feelings relating to the disapproving gaze of the public when their children did not meet normative standards of behaviour. This feeling of sadness and anger contributed to isolate and marginalize these women who experienced a huge lack of understanding and a great amount of ignorance in society. One important message from these mothers to the general public was, therefore, not to jump to conclusions when a child misbehaves. It might not necessarily be a 'bold' child who is not brought up properly by the mother, but in fact a child with special needs whose mother is doing the best she can. This stigma is closely associated with the socially constructed image of the 'good' mother who fulfils her maternal duties by presenting a 'perfectly behaved' child to the public. The mothers' stories strongly indicate that they experienced this stigma surrounding their ability to mother. They were judged in their roles by professionals, by people in the public, by other mothers of children with special needs and also by themselves. Many of the mothers, however, showed a resistance to being judged by others as 'bad' mothers. They were assertive and confident in their struggle to obtain services as a matter of right and often empowered by knowledge they had gained through sources like the Internet. Many of them were actively participating in support groups and campaigns where they voiced their views and opinions. This is also where a very interesting and important change in the gender divide took place. The mothers entered the public arena where their private lives became public issues, whereas the fathers, due to their reluctance to open up about their private feelings in groups, remained at home with the child. This change, I would argue, indicates that education and information are vital in order to support mothers of children with learning disabilities, who now have the courage to speak up and demand services as a matter of right. Furthermore, it reflects the cultural context in which they are living, where traditional values upheld by the state and the Roman Catholic Church are being questioned.

Finally, the Irish-born mothers strongly rejected the religious notions of 'being a special person given a special gift from God' as well as the child being 'a cross that has to be carried'. They experienced these comments as coming from people with no real knowledge about what it means to live with a child with special needs. Despite their sharp dismissal of these statements, many of the mothers described themselves as practising Catholics, albeit with reservations regarding the strength of their faith or the flaws of the church as an institution. Furthermore, most of the participants had liberal views 'the woman should be able to decide herself' regarding amniocentesis and abortions in cases where the child would have a severe disability. However, none of them would have opted for termination had they been given a choice.

In sum, this chapter has shown how Irish mothers of children with learning disabilities are designated and assume the role of the main carer and agent in a very gender divided society. Fathers are traditional breadwinners and provide much practical and emotional support, but leave the 'maternal worry and work' entirely to the mothers. This takes place in the context of a traditional, conservative society where prejudices and ignorance still dominate the field of disabilities. Mothers are slowly beginning to rebel against being labelled as 'bad' mothers and, empowered by knowledge and support groups, they stand up for the rights of the children. In the next and final chapter of this book I will draw together the themes raised in this book and discuss what we can learn from these maternal narratives.

Chapter 6

A Different Maternal Journey – Conclusion

This book has focused on the narratives of mothers of children with special needs. It has enabled us to see, in depth, how women like these make sense of this different maternal journey and adjust their lives accordingly. Eighteen mothers of children with Autistic Spectrum Disorder (ASD), Attention Deficit Hyperactivity Disorder (ADHD) and/or Down syndrome living in Ireland contributed to the book by telling their stories. This chapter draws together the themes raised in this book and explores the narratives in the context of theories on contemporary mothering. Although accounts of the lived experience of having a child with special needs already exist, few writers have so far explored this topic with a focus on the mother. Throughout this book I have stressed the importance of listening to what mothers have to say about themselves as subjects in their own right and how they reflect on their own thoughts and actions. This chapter will discuss these maternal reflections and use them in an attempt to find ways to better support this group of marginalized women in our society.

Life goes on: but with a difference

The experience of having a child with special needs is often one full of sadness and exhaustion. The narratives in this book are no exception as they contain many examples of hardship and pain suffered by the mothers. Despite large variations in the child's level of functioning and diagnosis, all mothers expressed similar feelings of stress and depression. The narratives also suggest that the actual type of disability is of less importance while considering stress factors. The day-to-day stress of living with a child with Down syndrome is similar to that of living with a child with high-functioning autism. This is in line with the theory that the child itself is not the main cause of grief and sadness but it is the lack of appropriate support from society that contributes to marginalize and isolate families living with learning disabilities (Buckley 2000; Case 2000; Murray 2000). The stories in this book also suggest that many mothers find various ways of coping and adapting to this new situation relatively soon. Their accounts then become counter-narratives to the medical model (Malacrida 2003) where professionals assume that mothers experience the child only as a burden. I do not dispute that the mother will always have a certain notion of sadness, as Mary said: 'the fun in you dies in one way'. But the child's physical presence and the need to care for this child force the mother to get on with her life: 'he just needed to be hugged and kissed and fed and changed and the rest of it' (Helen). Thus, instead of dwelling on the child that never was (the non-disabled child) mothers decide to focus on the child that is (the child with special needs): 'It's a very difficult thing...yes, it is terrible. But at the same time, here's this little life, you know' (Miriam). This positive focus, I believe, contributed to the mothers' willingness to tell their stories and they welcomed the opportunity to voice their experiences and be taken seriously.

Mothers' various positive coping strategies included attending parents' support groups and, if available, counselling. Many of the mothers emphasized the need for counselling, a service rarely offered by the professionals with whom they had contact. Similarly, the informal support from the participant's own mother was also many times highlighted as invaluable: 'My mother has just been my saviour' (Brenda). This shows that mothers felt most at ease when they could trust the care of their child to somebody close to them. Furthermore, mothers felt able to cope better if they knew that they could do something themselves in order to enhance the child's development: 'Once I got the ABA manual and there was something that I could actually do to help this child, then I was fine' (Julie). I will return to the satisfaction of this maternal work shortly. The degree of coping then was highly dependent on whether the mother's environment was supportive or not.

The experienced hardship was often due to patronizing attitudes from professionals such as paediatricians, psychiatrists, psychologists, social workers, teachers and school principals. Instead of feeling supported, the majority of the participants felt scrutinized and minimized in their roles as mothers. The lack of genuine partnerships between parents and professionals was apparent in all 18 narratives. Nowhere did the mothers have a substantial input in decisions regarding their child's education and independent living. This feeling was reflected in quotes such as these: 'I felt that I was treated coldly by the paediatrician...it's kind of him looking over his glasses, like "who are you telling me", you know' (Caitriona) and 'I said to her [social worker] Jonathan is my own child and you're telling me I can't have the information about him...and she said parents don't always understand these things' (Margaret). Although many accounts regarding the professionals were negative, positive support was also reported: 'Our social worker, now I must admit, for a couple of years, would have been certainly a great support' (Mary).

The lack of partnership in service-provision, I would argue, is due to the traditional top-down relationship that still exists in a culture where experts' knowledge is expected to be superior to that of the mothers. This inferiority complex is very noticeable in statements such as 'I know nothing, I'm only a mother', expressed by a mother participating in a television documentary on the lack of services for people with learning disabilities in Ireland (Prime Time Investigates 2004). The voices in this book, however, suggest that a new generation of mothers is challenging this power imbalance by becoming more assertive: 'There are no small gods, for want of a better word, anymore' (Mary). This challenge is manifested in different ways: one takes place in the 'battlefield' between mothers and professionals. The other is of a more subtle character where mothers ignore both the state and professionals and seek support elsewhere.

The 'war' with professionals: becoming resilient agents

Judging by the narratives of the mothers in this book, and also confirmed by other researchers (Read 1991, 2000; Read and Clements 2001; Redmond and Richardson 2003; Tarrant 2002; Todd and Jones 2003), the struggle for support and understanding seems inevitable and is often described in terms of 'war' or 'battle'. The mothers in this book reiterated these terms of conflict in the context of their relationship with professionals: 'It wasn't just a battle, it was a war' (Betty); 'the battle is on' (Helen); 'so then you take on the fighting of the system' (Mary). The majority of the mothers had taken on the role as agents for their children and engaged actively in lobbying politicians, chasing professionals and, in one case, going to court. The level of agency depended on how much resistance the mothers were meeting in their relationship with professionals. In few cases, where services were relatively satisfactory regarding the children's needs, the mothers' agency consisted of monitoring this current provision and maintaining a dialogue with teachers and therapists.

In most other circumstances, however, where there were little or no services at all, mothers were forced into more action (Read 2000). Judging by the narratives, it took time before the mothers felt assertive enough to express this resilience: 'it took a while to get that kind of pigheadedness into me' (Julie). This reflects the gradual change that takes place as the mother is forced to reconstruct her subjectivity. Mothers gradually adjust to this different maternal experience and it is also the most challenging time, as pointed out by McDonnell (1991, p.60). One of the mothers described this experience: 'Initially it [the diagnosis] was a shock...but after the initial two months of terror, I was kind of glad it was something there and it wasn't me...but it was like, oh, my God, I have to start a whole new way and I have to learn about this now.' (Mary).

The mothers in this book indicated that professionals' unhelpful attitudes triggered strong responses: 'I wouldn't lie down as easy...I got stronger from them' (Julie), 'I have no fear at all...I wouldn't care now' (Betty). I also sensed this resilience in the narrative of the least 'rebellious' mother. Therese first stated that she found professionals' expertise superior. However, reflecting on it, she changed her mind: 'the way I was brought up, you did as you were told, and these people know what they're talking about, well, in actual fact I've learned that people don't know what they're talking about. I know a lot more than they do' (Therese). Therese's narrative, however, indicates that there are many mothers who do not openly challenge professionals. They might have other more personal and acute problems to deal with, such as poverty and abuse. Some women, however, choose a different way of showing their resilience. In doing so, they rely on their own expertise as mothers and intensify this maternal work under extraordinary circumstances.

Extraordinary mothering: an alternative resilience?

Some of the mothers in this book had chosen alternative ways of dealing with archaic social policies and educational provisions. Their resilience did not involve confrontations with service-providers and professionals. Instead, these mothers decided to spend their time and energy on their own children, ignoring the lack of support from the state. Paradoxically, the sense of being left with little or no support at all, forced some mothers to take the control themselves: 'I figured, well, I can look after him myself' (Martina); 'I have to concentrate on my own child now' (Miriam); 'I'd go down that road again with John...he has made such a progress' (Julie). These mothers chose to engage full time in extraordinary maternal work instead of wasting time waiting for outside help. Mothers of non-disabled children invest a lot of this maternal thinking and work in the early days of the child's development. Ruddick's (1989) definition of this maternal work is helpful in order to understand why mothers make this choice. According to Ruddick, the basis for the maternal work is maternal thinking. This thinking is evoked by the child's need to be 'protected, nurtured and trained' (p.23). However, as this child becomes more independent and trained, the mother can begin to let go. This is particularly true when the children reach school age and the state shares the responsibility for the child's education. Many mothers of children with learning disabilities, on the other hand, are forced to provide this extra support for their children. The main reason for this, I would argue, is the lack of service provision. The vast majority of the mothers in this book spent hours doing this extraordinary maternal work with their children. The amount of time and the type of work involved, however, varied depending on the circumstances. For mothers of children with severe and moderate learning disabilities, the maternal work invested was similar to that of watching over toddlers. Mothers of children with high-functioning disabilities, on the other hand, focused on social skills training and behaviour.

Ten out of the eighteen mothers had given up their employment in order to be at home full time. Four of these mothers felt happier to stay at home than to continue to work and this decision had little to do with the fact that they had a child with special needs. Two mothers were happy to stay at home while the children were young, but planned to return to work at a later stage. Four mothers had given up their work because of their children with special needs, but expressed little or no regret regarding this lack of choice. This surprised me, as I expected to encounter feelings of resentment and bitterness relating to this experience. On the contrary, the decision to remain at home was looked upon favourably by the majority of the mothers and I believe that there are several explanations to this. First, these mothers were in a financially secure position to stay at home as they had breadwinning partners. Second, the mothers felt that their maternal work, consisting of training and educating their own children, was rewarding in itself: 'I've gained as much from them as I've given' (Brenda), 'I'd go down that road again with John...because there's nothing like the [feeling]' (Julie). For these two mothers in particular, their maternal work changed the lives of their children. Brenda's daughters and Julie's son had been 'written off' by professionals as autistic with severe learning disabilities. After years of intensive training at home, these children proved the expertise wrong and become high-functioning individuals in mainstream. This high level of investment in maternal thinking and work also reflects changes in the mother's subjectivity, and I will return to this discussion later in this chapter.

The mothers' preferences to perform maternal work did not reduce them to passive dependants confined silently to the private sphere. Instead of looking for support from professionals and the state, they turned to other sources of information. The Internet played a vital role for many mothers in their search for new ways to train and educate their children. Others discovered new teaching methods by consulting literature on alternative therapies. This active search for information and subsequent acquired knowledge changes the power dynamics between mothers and professionals radically. Although the actual mothering still takes place in the confinement of the home, the private sphere, the boundaries are changing. By entering the public sphere of the Internet from home, a new generation of mothers are empowered to meet professionals at a different level compared to in the past. This newly gained knowledge is also spread and shared within parents' support groups and organizations, contributing to a sense of assertiveness. Thus this new access to the public world of expertise makes it easier for mothers to move in and out of the private and public spheres as 'active social agents' (Ribbens 1994, pp.205–6). Mothers rarely expressed negative feelings towards the actual maternal work they engaged in. Instead, the anger was directed towards the state for not providing mothers with a real choice. Margaret, for example, had given up her 'grand plan' of combining a career with motherhood and said it was hard to have 'missed the boat'. Nevertheless, she felt that this was a sacrifice she had to do in order for the family to function. In her eyes, nobody else could do her job of mothering four children with high-functioning autism. But instead of resenting her children's disabilities and her personal limited choices, Margaret attacked the government and its family policy. She felt discriminated against for being at home full time and called for financial recognition of the maternal work involved in nurturing children with special needs. Another mother, Marie, reacted against the presumption that all women today want to combine a career with motherhood. In this sense, she felt that her son's disability allowed her the choice of staying at home, albeit admitting that it was no real choice. These mothers called for the state to value the care they provided for their children.

Mothers in paid employment portrayed an extremely difficult situation trying to combine a career with motherhood. Two of them, for example, who were in full-time employment and main breadwinners expressed a wish to cut down work hours. Although they enjoyed their work, they were still main agents for their children and experienced huge amounts of stress trying to do both. In these two cases, financial circumstances forced the mothers to work. Not all mothers in this book, however, were prepared to sacrifice their career in order to meet the needs of the child. Trish, for example, resented the fact that her child's disability prevented her from working full time: 'I'm working to get away from him…it's not even for the money.' As a single young mother, Trish's personal circumstances differed in many ways from the majority of the participants who were married to breadwinning partners. Like Trish, Anne experienced huge difficulties in finding suitable childcare for her son and consequently decided to give up her work. In Anne's case, the loss of income for the family was the main cause for worry. These narratives suggest that as the family pattern changes in Ireland, more choices will have to be available in the form of care provision. The reality today is that there are very few choices available for mothers like Trish who really have to and want to participate in the workforce full time. Whereas it is of utmost importance to value the mother's care and reward it financially, it will not empower women who do not want to or who are not able to do this care full time. Other services, such as childcare and out-of-school care, are needed to provide these women with a real choice and appropriate support. I argue, however, that the quality of these services must be guided by standards set by mothers.

Sharing the care with the mother

There is a strong notion in this book suggesting that if the mothers did not do the maternal work themselves, nobody else would do it. This notion was expressed in statements like these: 'If I don't keep on top of it, nobody is going to do it. So I just got to do it' (Mary); 'If I didn't [work with him] where would he be, you know, there's no one else… It's a full-time job' (Mary); 'If I had gone out to work, what would have become of my son' (Julie) and 'I'm his mother, like if I'm not going to do it, who is going to do it?' (Margaret). These mothers had set certain standards of care and education related to their children's needs. As the state failed to provide similar standards of service provision, they were forced to do it themselves. Differences in the children's level of functioning sometimes determined the level of outside support needed by the mothers. Two mothers of children with moderate to severe learning disabilities had fought hard for regular respite services and succeeded because of legal intervention: 'I would be dead without it' (Caitriona). Similarly, these mothers saw the need for future residential care for their children. They felt, however, that unless there was a radical change in service provisions, their children would more than likely remain at home with them as long as they were able to care for them. This feeling of resignation was even more evident in the narratives of the mothers of children with Asperger syndrome and ADHD. It appeared unthinkable for these mothers that other people could or would share the extraordinary maternal support with them. The majority of these mothers, however, would have preferred it if services were in place to assist them in this work.

The mothers' willingness and preference to be main caregivers did not exclude demands for assistance and support. One of my participants had benefited from 'distributed mothering', as defined by Kittay (1999, p.13). Mary, mother of Patrick, diagnosed autistic with a severe learning disability, spoke about her sense of ease as others took over her work: 'I'm much happier because I know Patrick is getting it, and I know it's stuff Patrick loves...and he's also progressing with this bit of support' (Mary). Community-based staff cannot be expected to share the mother's love for the child, as they do not share the same maternal motivation for the work involved. The aim should nevertheless be to provide this maternal care as far as it is possible. In order to establish this form of community care, we first need to create an awareness of the concept of sharing the maternal work, as discussed in this book. More education and training is needed, both for staff working directly with people with disabilities, but also for policy makers and legislators. There are no doubt many difficulties with this approach. One is the practical nature of caregiving work as employment in comparison to lifelong mothering. Whereas the mother usually follows the child throughout many of his or her different stages in life, staff will come and go. Thus, the mother feels compelled to hold a firm grip, as only she knows the full story. A lack of understanding of the mother's firm grip can contribute to her being dismissed by professionals as over-anxious or militant. One of my participants, for example, expressed this feeling of being judged by professionals, as she asked to read a report on her child: 'I sometimes think they think I'm hysterical...' (Margaret). In extreme cases, mothers can be accused of not acting in the best interest of the child and I will return to the theme of 'bad' mothering later. These conflicts can be prevented by maintaining an ongoing communication between everyone concerned. In practical terms, this means introducing genuine partnerships regarding social policies and service provisions for children with special needs.

The word 'partnership' has been used extensively in research on families living with disabilities (Case 2000; Dale 1996; Knox *et al.* 2000; Murray

2000; Sloper 1999). In order to avoid the term becoming a cliché, the meaning behind a true partnership has to be spelled out, and more importantly, it has to be implemented. A partnership begins by professionals listening to mothers and taking their views seriously. This was also the most striking message the mothers in this study had for professionals: 'Do not minimize parents, listen to what they're saying' (Margaret) and 'Treat me as an equal... We're not stupid' (Caitriona). Listening is, however, not enough. I argue that a true partnership entails mothers and professionals involved together, on equal terms, in planning and implementing services. In a genuine partnership, mothers should have the right to the same financial and organizational power as the service provider or policy maker. Mothers should be able to invite professionals to discuss future plans for their children with them, rather than professionals inviting the mothers to attend their round table talks. Another way of looking at this relationship would be for mothers to consider themselves as consumers, shopping around for preferred services (Buckley 2000; Pillinger 2002). Whereas many of my participants would welcome that level of involvement, it might not be the case for all mothers, or indeed fathers. Nevertheless, I believe that a new assertive generation of parents will eventually change this situation and be encouraged to participate in decision-making. Under these different circumstances, the expertise of the mother will not be perceived by the professionals as a threat, but instead as a valuable contribution. Similarly, if policy makers and service providers fully understand mothers' needs and provide necessary support, mothers should not have to become 'thorns' or 'arrows' in their sides. More importantly, in order to bring mothers and professionals closer together, I believe that we all need to examine our internalized notions of motherhood and mothering. How do we expect mothers of children with special needs to behave? What maternal narratives are acceptable in our modern society?

The social construction of motherhood

The most striking commonality amongst the women in this book was the mothers' acceptance of their roles as mothers first and foremost and their commitment to their children. Their own wellbeing was solely discussed in the context of their children's wellbeing, regardless of whether it entailed the present or the future. When these mothers expressed a need for support from society, it was with the aim to help the child or to allow the mother to spend time with other children in the family. It appeared to me that mothers were reluctant to speak of their own personal needs as it could be judged as selfish and unnatural. This was evident in one mother's narrative relating to her decision to embark on a career as a speech therapist: 'there's a whole future ahead of me, where there wouldn't have been, which sounds awfully selfish, but there is because of him, and he has sparked that interest, which is great' (Martina). Another mother expressed the same sentiment when she wanted time on her own instead of devoting herself to her other children: 'When he is in respite I try and give that time to them [the other children], or if I'm selfish and say, look it's my day, they won't get the time.' (Caitriona).

The majority of the mothers also emphasized the importance of the role of the father and many times praised his emotional support and practical input. None of the 18 mothers, however, shared the maternal thinking and work, as defined by Ruddick (1989), with the fathers. The fathers' input was instead related to hands-on activities: 'Father is the great fun' (Martina). Even in the case where the mother was the main breadwinner, the father's input was limited to being practical: 'He's the one that gets him up in the mornings' (Margaret). The maternal thinking and worry seemed, according to the narrators, to mainly be the mother's responsibility. Thus the mothers alone chased professionals and read relevant information on the child's disability and various treatments. Some mothers resented this heavy workload: 'So you feel that you're carrying the whole lot' (Mary). The majority of the mothers, however, expressed no anger whatsoever towards the fathers' lack of 'mental' involvement. This finding was surprising, as I expected to encounter more negativity regarding the mothers' relationship with the fathers. The only two mothers seriously criticizing the father's lack of involvement were single. A third mother had experienced marital difficulties, but this had nothing to do with their child with special needs. The remaining 15 mothers had overwhelmingly positive things to say about the fathers. One explanation to this could be the mothers' reluctance to fully open up and reveal their private lives to me. Most of them, I believe, wanted to talk about their children only. They preferred to keep other private aspects of their lives to themselves. Another explanation, however, is related to the cultural context in which these mothers were living. I believe that within this small group of mothers, the role divide between the mother and the father was genuinely positively experienced and not questioned. Even in the cases where the mothers were single, the division of labour had never been an issue. This internalized notion of the mother's gendered role in society is deeply rooted, not only in Ireland, but also elsewhere in the world. This could explain why Swedish mothers of children with special needs, despite high level of state support by international standards, score high on scales of stress and depression in comparison to fathers and mothers of non-disabled children (Olsson 2004). Many Swedish mothers of children with learning disabilities give up their careers, as the double workload becomes too much for them. As working is the norm in Sweden, they find it hard to adjust to full-time motherhood (Olsson and Hwang 2003, p.338). Irish women, on the other hand, are living in a culture where many mothers are still traditional homemakers. This cultural difference, I would argue, can explain why the women in this book did not reflect much on their roles as mothers, vis-à-vis the fathers.

In the socially constructed role of the mother, as Dalley (1996) points out, women are expected to both 'care for', doing the actual physical work with the child, as well as 'care about' the child's progress and future. Society takes this for granted, and so did the mothers in my study. The father's support mainly consisted of support in the form of 'caring about', or providing for the family financially. In the families where the father did as much of the 'caring for' as the mother, the main task of 'caring about' was still the responsibility of the mother. Paradoxically, one mother felt supported by her husband's lack of worries: 'His answer to everything was, "Julie, he'll be OK, he'll be OK" (Julie). The socially constructed role of the father, according to Waltzer (1996), is to tell the mother not to worry. This was also evident in my narratives: 'I'd say my fears to my husband, 'oh, sure he'll be alright, he'll be alright', but I think [he said so] to try and quell my fears...' (Mary). I cannot claim to speak on behalf of fathers, as this book does not involve their narratives. My discussion then is based on how the mothers experienced and viewed the role of the fathers. It is quite clear, however, that the father's employment status did not change because of the child's special needs. Furthermore, his role as a father did not appear to be under the same scrutiny as the mother. She faced most of these challenges, and consequently had to adjust to a different reality of motherhood and reconstruct her subjectivity.

Reconstructing maternal subjectivities

How then did the mothers reconstruct their subjectivities and make sense of this different maternal journey? Many of them became 'extraordinary' mothers caring for their children, as already mentioned. This personal sacrifice did evoke anger directed towards the state and also at the Catholic Church as an institution. There was a particular denouncement of religious comments such as 'a cross that has to be carried', or 'a special gift from God'. It was within this religious context that mothers appeared to reconstruct their identities with force. They rebelled against the notion that they were specially chosen and passive recipients of this 'heavenly gift'. The vast majority dismissed these statements as 'utterly rubbish' (Margaret), 'crap' (Margaret) or 'the Irish way to deal with a hurtful situation' (Caitriona). Some of the mothers claimed, however, that the child itself had brought a gift to the mother. This gift consisted of opening up a new world of opportunities. Martina, for example, embarked on an academic career aiming to become a speech therapist: 'He has sparked that interest.' I would argue that this alternative gift-rhetoric, as discussed by Landsman (1999), assisted the mothers in their struggle to reconstruct their identities. This struggle took place in a culture which has a strong notion of the 'good' mother. This is, in my opinion, deeply internalized in Western society and it was reflected in the way the mothers considered themselves.

The normative motherhood discourse creates a mother-blaming culture, which is especially hard on single mothers, teenage mothers, lesbian mothers, coloured mothers and poor mothers. Even the married heterosexual mother of a non-disabled child will experience guilt as she tries to combine a career with fulfilling the role of a being a good mother (O'Reilly 2006). Does her child receive the same maternal nurture in the childcare setting as it does at home? Do the staff really understand what she feels is important in her child's life? Mothers of children with special needs share these worries, often in magnified proportions. This is particularly true for mothers of children with autism or ADHD who, in the public gaze, look perfectly non-disabled but have severe behaviour problems. These mothers are scrutinized and judged by people in their surroundings, including extended families, and as a consequence they withdraw from the public sphere and become isolated. This book suggests that the most hurtful experience took place in public places where mothers were held responsible for their children's behaviour. Many met this challenge by leaving immediately: 'You just bite your tongue, like, and just take him away' (Mary); 'We would just leave' (Brenda); 'All I could do was...just put him in the car and drive home' (Caitriona). Mothers of children with Down syndrome also encountered negative attitudes, especially while trying to enrol their children in mainstream schools: 'Down syndrome – snotty nose and frothing of the mouth' (Helen).

It was in circumstances like these that women's lives changed dramatically, due to raising a child with special needs. This was when manuals on childrearing were of no use and mothers felt alienated from the normative discourse of motherhood. Thus these negative encounters forced the mothers into reconstructing their maternal subjectivities in various ways. Some of them recreated motherhood as a 'social activist position' (McDonnell 1991, p.73) and turned their personal suffering into positive action, in order to help others in similar situations. This experience was evident in the narrative of one mother when she explained her reason for setting up a parents' support group: 'All I wanted was just to help other people who were maybe going through a similar situation or to make sure that nobody ever went through what I went through' (Caitriona). I believe that this is a way for mothers to find a place for themselves in this new world of mothering. Thus, two of the mothers in this book were founders of parents' support groups, and several others were actively involved in similar organizations. As the mother accepts that she cannot change the child, she sets out to change the world (McDonnell 1991, p.73).

Other mothers, however, struggled to normalize the child. This involved the already mentioned extraordinary level of maternal work that they invested in the children. Mothers then made huge personal sacrifices in order to support their children to become accepted as members of society. This had little to do with the mothers' denial of the child's disability and not accepting the child's values. Instead, the uncertainty of the child's future and the potential benefits in fostering the growth of the child, spurred the mothers to do this sacrifice. Miriam, for example, hoped that teaching her son William at home full time would benefit him in the future: 'If I put in a lot of effort now, [I hoped that] it would actually save me a lot of effort later.' Paradoxically, this commitment to maternal work forced many mothers deeper into the socially constructed role of the mother. As a consequence, they judged themselves in the light of being the 'good' mother who, to a certain extent, becomes a martyr for her child. My participants saw their mothering as part of their identities, and did not reflect upon it as being extraordinary. This internalized view of motherhood contributes to glorify women like Marie O'Donoghue and Kathy Sinnott who took on the Irish state in order to fight for their children (see Chapter 2). Without minimizing their personal struggles and achievements it is tempting to question what would have happened if they had fought for the sake of themselves and their own rights? I have no doubt that a different attitude would have lessened the public sympathy enormously. It is also highly unlikely that a court case could have been taken arguing on behalf of the mother's right to participate in society on equal terms with other citizens.

Thus the unspoken rule of a mother's unselfishness has serious consequences for mothers caring for children with disabilities. These mothers feel compelled to cope with their expected maternal duties and do so until they virtually collapse. Paradoxically, some mothers choose to remain silent. In their eyes seeking support from the outside is seen as a failure and thus often resisted. One participant in my study expressed this feeling of not wanting to appear to be helpless in the eyes of professionals: 'I didn't want to look like some "God help her"' (Marie). Although most mothers, such as Marie, usually broke this first level of 'self-enforced' silence after some time and began demanding services for their children, their were certain aspects of their lives that they remained silent about (Greenspan 1998, pp.43–4). They rarely acknowledged their own needs and aspirations, perhaps afraid of being, yet again, considered bad and selfish mothers. This second level of self-silencing became even more evident during the feedback process as it took the form of self-censoring. Two mothers returned the manuscripts of their interviews and asked me to omit parts that portrayed their mothering in a negative way. Another mother admitted having negative feelings towards her child and sometimes wishing that he never had been born. While saying this, she immediately expressed guilt for having such sentiments in the first place: 'It's a terrible thing to say and it's an awful thing, like as regards the mother... I mean this is an alien thing to a mother to say like that...' (Mary). Thus, admitting feelings such as these were considered signs of 'bad' mothering.

The ambivalence of mothering

As the mothers focused on their children, educating them and fighting for them, they felt confident as 'good' mothers. The credibility of their stories is, I would argue, even stronger as many of them had the courage to reveal their maternal ambivalences. Their relationship with their children was not always rose-tinted. Some of the mothers spoke frankly about how they dealt with their own anger directed at their children. Margaret's first-born son, for example, screamed 24 hours a day: ' I would have strangled him if I hadn't breastfed him...then when he weaned...I used to put him in the cot, when I felt that he was under threat...I just dumped him in the cot and ran out, I ran downstairs so at least he was safe.' Similarly, Mary went to her GP for help as she felt that her son's behaviour would force her to physically attack him. Another mother, Anne, smashed a pizza into her son's face as he threw it on the floor. These women were not afraid of telling these stories, as they wanted their vulnerable situation to be taken seriously. Furthermore, they had remained in reasonable control of their anger and they had never seriously abused their children.

This maternal ambivalence, however, raises important issues for professionals involved in supporting these families. Featherstone (1999) urges social workers to be aware of volatile relationships between mothers and children in general. They need to fully understand the circumstances and listen to mothers who are crying out for help. One of the mothers had, for example, begged social workers to place her son in care. Trish's son had physically attacked her and she felt that she could not cope any longer. The social workers, however, could not help Trish, as the child was not considered at risk. If mothering were taken seriously, Trish would perhaps have received the support she needed. Paradoxically, Helen came under hard scrutiny as she admitted to smacking her son: 'How do you smack him? Where do you smack him? With what do you do it?' Helen was, in the eyes of the professionals, a 'bad' mother who did not act in her child's best interest. It is under circumstances like these that the real power imbalance between mothers and professionals is revealed. Smacking a child is, I would argue, culturally accepted in Ireland. Professionals, such as my GP and a neurosurgeon who my son attended, advised me as a mother to smack my child in order to make him behave. In their role as professionals, and probably as fathers of non-disabled children, their views and perhaps actions regarding smacking their own children would probably never come under professional scrutiny. In Helen's case however, the smacking was considered to reflect 'bad' mothering by the multi-disciplinary team involved in her son's case. This professional scrutiny of 'good' or 'bad' mothering can also increase the resistance among mothers.

Similarly, mothers of children with special needs and professionals become involved in a 'truth game' (Malacrida 2003, p.231). In this game, mothers claim to know the truth regarding their children's condition and wellbeing. Professionals, in turn, based on their expertise claim to have the same knowledge. Professionals have, however, the ultimate power, controlling service provisions such as education and respite care and mothers have to restrict their resistance to a certain extent if they want their children to remain in the system. Revealing stories of maternal ambivalence is therefore brave and these women are at risk of being judged by society as incompetent and unfit mothers. In order to avoid this scrutiny, many choose to remain silent. Judging by recent events in Ireland, it can be argued that there is a real risk facing outspoken parents who come under the scrutiny of professionals. Padraig and Mary O'Hara, for example, had their four children diagnosed with autism taken into care against their will after they protested publicly against lack of services (Prime Time Investigates 2004). Local health authorities argued that the children were at risk at home as the parents were not coping. However, a court ordered the return of the children to their parents after a week in care but only when the mother agreed to undergo a psychiatric assessment (O'Brien 2005b; 2005c). This particular case clearly illustrates the risks involved in revealing private worries in public and contributes to silencing vulnerable mothers (and indeed fathers) in need of support.

Professionals are not the only actors in this 'mother-blaming' game. Mothers also blame each other as well as themselves for failing to be 'good' mothers. This happens both in the normative world of mothering, as well as within the world of mothering special needs. I believe that there is even more increased pressure on the mother of a child with a learning disability to find the best training and therapies available. In the never-ending flow of new methods and promising therapies and drugs, the mother has to make difficult decisions relating to her own child's education and care. The mothers in this book who devoted themselves entirely to their own children had experienced blame for being selfish and not considering society as a whole: 'that other mum said to me, "sometimes Julie, you were blindfolded in one way – John, John, John. John got every single thing". But I did and I apologize to no one for that' (Julie); 'she [another mum] was sort of like attacking me for doing this [teaching the child] and it was like if this was the answer...why wasn't I out there telling everyone?' (Miriam). Many mothers had also experienced the dilemma of making decisions concerning their children's needs and struggled with a guilty conscience. Margaret, for example, sometimes felt guilty for not working harder with her son: 'Should I be pushing him more? I think, God, is she a better mother than me?' Margaret's dilemma was, I would argue, not a unique experience. What is unique, however, is to voice this particular maternal experience and discuss it openly.

Conclusion

Mothering special needs entails embarking on a different maternal journey, often complicated and full of twists. Although this journey differs from one individual to another, depending on various social, cultural and material circumstances, there are also many similarities. The most important similarity is that the vast majority of these mothers continue their extraordinary maternal work while at the same time try to live up to society's expectations of 'good' mothers. The purpose of this book is to challenge this socially constructed role of motherhood and widen the repertoire of possible story lines (Miller 2005). By encouraging mothers to speak of their own needs and aspirations, without imposing any moral judgements, we can bring their concerns higher up on the public agenda.

The mothers in this book stressed how much they appreciated talking to a researcher who knew the experience of mothering a child with special needs: 'It was good to tell my story to people who understood' (Therese); 'I needed to tell my story to somebody willing to listen and somebody who understood where I was coming from' (Mary). As I asked mothers for feedback on the research process, many of them appeared to be supported by reading what others had said: 'I felt when reading it that it was all about me, even though I know other people were interviewed but it all touches home. Thank you' (Anne); 'I think you hit the nail on the head – our stories are similar in so many ways – we can all relate to each other stories' (Catriona). Similarly, their expectations of the published work were great: 'I hope this research will be read by all the professionals and it will enlighten them' (Mary) and 'a copy should be forwarded to the service providers' (Helen). These high expectations worried me for two reasons. First, what they had read and commented on, a short summary of initial interpretations, was only a fraction of the final work and I am fully aware of the risk that some of the mothers may feel that their words and views have been misrepresented. All I can do is hope that they will be able to identify with and feel positive about the end result. Second, this small-scale study might go unnoticed in the world of professionals who do not consider these narratives worthy of attention. However, I hope this dismissal of maternal voices will change as more social scientific research on motherhood/mothering is undertaken (Miller 2005, p.159).

Finally, I hope that mothers of children with special needs who read this book will feel encouraged to openly tell their stories, not only as mothers but also as individuals with needs of their own. I believe that sharing maternal stories, depicting various different lived experiences in relation to children with special needs, can provide some comfort and support. Although mothers will continue to buy books on therapies, methods and treatments for their children in order to improve their children's lives, we need more books revealing personal accounts about mothers themselves (Deckmar 2005). We also need to support mothers who, for various reasons, cannot help their children on their own and who cannot cope with this different maternal journey. This specific support for mothers could be provided through local peer-led self-help groups and also within larger national disability organizations.

Furthermore, the Internet has brought the world into our private homes and there are already numerous websites providing support and advice for families. These websites usually deal with a specific learning disability or, in the context of mothering of non-disabled children, general parenting support. There is, I believe, a need for a website designed for the purpose of supporting mothers of children with various special needs. This could be undertaken as a joint venture between mothers and professionals together, challenging a society that so far has taken mothering for granted.

Epilogue

The day I decided to write this book was the day I began to make sense of my different maternal journey. Until that day I had put my own life on a shelf while going through the process of denial, shock, grief and gradual acceptance of my child's special needs. With the support of other mothers in the same situation I began focusing on myself and what to do with my life now that the original mothering journey was disrupted. Researching for and writing this book then became my way of coping with the rollercoaster trip my son brought me on. One thing that I learnt along the way is that this maternal journey never stays the same, but it is constantly changing. The passengers are also unique individuals with diverse political, religious and cultural beliefs, albeit on the same journey. For some, the enthusiasm and energy to improve the child's cognitive or social skills might fade as the years go by. Others finally meet people who really listen and support them in doing whatever can be done to help the child. Sometimes all we mothers need, in order to have a life of our own, is this bit of extra support.

While I was writing this book my son, now a broad-shouldered teenager, achieved many things that I never thought possible. I credit myself, his father and sister – and most of all himself – for some of this progress. We still have very low moments too. I do not blame myself or anyone else when that happens. These moments are part of my particular maternal journey – unique to me but quite similar to others in many ways.

Appendix: Profile of Participants

(At the time of the first interview – all names have been changed.)

Mary is a mother of four. Her eldest son Patrick has a severe learning disability and autism. She is a former childcare worker and restaurant employee, but works at home full time now. Her husband is a farmer.

Miriam is a mother of three. Her youngest son William has Down syndrome. She runs a business with her husband, but is now working full time teaching William at home.

Helen is a mother of three. Her youngest son Andrew has Down syndrome. Helen is a former office employee, but works at home full time now. Her husband is in a managerial position in a large international company.

Julie is a mother of two and her youngest son John is diagnosed having high-functioning autism. She works full time at home and her husband is self-employed.

Margaret has four children diagnosed with autistic spectrum disorder aged 6 to 17. Margaret is a writer but has given up her career to work at home full time. She is married to an engineer.

Marie has three children and her middle son Eoin has a severe learning disability and autism. Marie, formerly a self-employed therapist, works at home full time. Her husband is in a managerial position in a financial institution.

Martina is a mother of three children and her eldest son Daniel has been diagnosed with Asperger syndrome. Martina, formerly a bank official, works at home full time. Her husband is an employee in a financial institution.

Anne is a mother of three children and her middle son Noel has been diagnosed with Asperger syndrome and Attention Deficit Hyperactivity Disorder (ADHD). Anne, a former shop-manager, works at home full time. She is married to a civil servant.

Brenda is a mother of four children and her two youngest daughters Sally and Susan are diagnosed with Asperger syndrome. Brenda, a former interior designer, is separated and works at home full time.

Marie is a mother of two children and her eldest son Kevin is diagnosed with Asperger syndrome. Marie, a former teacher, works at home full time and her husband is self-employed.

Margaret is a mother of three children and her youngest son Jonathan has Down syndrome and ADHD. She works full time in the public sector and her husband is a casual part-time worker.

Mary is a mother of two children and her youngest son Patrick is diagnosed with ADHD. She is in full-time employment within the health board and her husband is a casual part-time worker.

Betty is a mother of three and her youngest son Michael has Down syndrome. A former office employee, she now works at home full time and is married to a dairy farmer.

Laura is a mother of two, her youngest son Kevin is diagnosed with autism. Laura works part time in the IT-business and her husband is an employee in an international company.

Caitriona is a mother of three children. Her youngest son Donnacha is diagnosed autistic with a moderate learning disability. Caitriona used to work as a childminder, but now works part time for a parents' organization. Her husband is self-employed.

Therese is a mother of three. Her middle son John is diagnosed with Asperger syndrome. Therese is self-employed and works from home. Her husband is also self-employed.

Trish is a single mother of Robert, who is diagnosed as having ADHD. Trish works part time as an office employee.

Mary is a single mother of Donal who is diagnosed with Asperger syndrome. She works part time in an employment scheme.

Useful Contacts

The list below is limited and I welcome anyone to contact me directly for further contact details: email: kajsa@iol.ie or postal address: Knockalisheen, Togher, Cork, Ireland. All websites were accessed 28 February 2007.

CHADD
America's national resource centre for Children and Adults with Attention Deficit Hyperactivity Disorder.

CHADD National Office
8181 Professional Place – Suite 150
Landover
Maryland 20785
USA
Phone: +1 301 306 7070
www.chadd.org

Thanet ADDERS ADD/ADHD support group
45 Vincent Close
Broadstairs
Kent CT10 2ND
UK
Phone: +44 (0)8709 503 693
www.adders.org

The National Autistic Society
393 City Road
London
EC1V 1NG
UK
Phone: +44 (0)20 7833 2299
www.nas.org.uk

Irish Autism Action
41 Newlands
Mullingar
Co. Westmeath
Ireland
Phone: +353 4 4933 1609
www.autismireland.ie

The Autism Council of Australia Ltd
41 Cook St
PO Box 361
Forestville NSW 2087
Australia
Phone: +61 2 8977 8300
www.autismaus.com.au/aca/

Autism Society of America
7910 Woodmont Avenue, Suite 300
Bethesda
Maryland 20814-3067
USA
Phone: +1 301 657 0881
www.autism-society.org

ASPIRE
Asperger Syndrome Association of Ireland
Aspire Main Office
Coleraine House
Carmichael Centre
Coleraine Street
Dublin 7
Ireland
Phone: +353 1 878 0027 or 878 0029
www.aspire-irl.org

National Down Syndrome Congress
1370 Center Drive, Suite 102
Atlanta
Georgia 303 38
USA
Phone: +1 800 232 NDSC (6372)
www.ndsccenter.org

Down's Syndrome Association
Langdon Down Centre
2a Langdon Park
Teddington TW11 9PS
UK
Phone: +44 (0)845 230 0372
www.downs-syndrome.org.uk

Down Syndrome Ireland
30 Mary Street
Dublin 1
Ireland
Phone: +353 1 873 0999
www.downsyndrome.ie

Worldwide support network for Down syndrome
www.downsyndrome.com

Motherhood/Mothering contacts

Association for Research on Mothering (ARM)
726 Atkinson
York University
4700 Keele Street
Toronto ON M3J 1P3
Canada
Phone: +1 416 736 2100 x60366
www.yorku.ca/crm

www.motherblogs.net

This is a website where women can write about anything and everything that has to do with motherhood/mothering

www.mothersmovement.org
This website provides resources and reporting for mothers and others who think about social change

Books by Mothers of Children with Special Needs

Addison, A. (2003) *One Small Starfish: A Mother's Everyday Advice, Survival Tactics and Wisdom for Raising a Special Needs Child.* Arlington, Texas: Future Horizons Inc.

Beck, M. (1999) *Expecting Adam: A True Story of Birth, Rebirth and Everyday Magic.* New York: Random House Inc.

Callahan, M. (1987) *Fighting for Tony.* New York: Simon & Schuster.

Clairborne Park, C. (2001) *Exiting Nirvana.* Boston: Bach Bay Books: Little Brown.

De Clercq, H. (2000) *Mum, is that a Human Being or an Animal? A Book on Autism.* Bristol: Lucky Duck Publishing.

Edgar, J. (1999) *Love, Hope and Autism.* London: The National Autistic Society.

Fletcher, J. (1996, 2000) *Marching to a Different Tune: Diary about an ADHD Boy.* London:Jessica Kingsley Publishers.

Fling, E.R. (2000) *Eating an Artichoke: A Mother's Perspective on Aspergers Syndrome.* London: Jessica Kingsley Publishers.

Gill, B. (1998) *Changed by a Child: Companion Notes for Parents of a Child with a Disability.* New York: Doubleday.

Gregory, J. (1996) *Bringing Up a Challenging Child at Home: When Love is Not Enough.* London: Jessica Kingsley Publishers.

Hocking, B. (1990) *Little Boy Lost: My Autistic Son.* London: Bloomsbury Publishers Ltd.

Holland, O. (2002) *The Dragons of Autism: Autism as a Source of Wisdom.* London: Jessica Kingsley Publishers.

Marsh, J. (ed.) (1995) *From the Heart: On Being a Mother of a Child With Special Needs.* Maryland: Woodbine House Publishing.

Vredevelt, P. (1998) *Angel Behind the Rocking Chair: Stories of Hope in Unexpected Places.* Oregon: Multnomah Publishers Inc.

References

Abberley, P. (2002) 'Work, Disability, Disabled People and European Social Theory.' In C. Barnes, M. Oliver and L. Barton (eds) *Disability Studies Today.* Cambridge: Polity Press.

Abbey, S. and O'Reilly, A. (eds) (1998) *Redefining Motherhood: Changing Identities and Patterns.* Toronto: Second Story Press.

Ainbinder, J.G., Blanchard, L.W., Singer, G.H.S., Sullivan, M.E., Powers, L.K., Marquis, J.G., Santelly, B. and the Consortium to Evaluate Parent to Parent (1998) 'A Qualitative Study of Parent to Parent Support for Parents of Children with Special Needs.' *Journal of Pediatric Psychology 23,* 2, 99–109.

All-Party Oireachtas Committee on the Constitution (2005) *Constitution Review Group Report: The Family.* Dublin: Stationery Office.

Amnesty International (2002) 'Mental Illness Campaign Unveiled.' *Amnesty Ireland 118,* 14.

Attwood, T. (1998) *Asperger Syndrome: A Guide for Parents and Professionals.* London: Jessica Kingsley Publishers.

Baldwin, S. and Carlisle, J. (1994) *Social Support for Disabled Children and their Families. A Review of the Literature.* Edinburgh: Social Work Services Inspectorate.

Ballard, K., Bray, A., Shelton, E.J. and Clarkson, J. (1997) 'Children with Disabilities and the Education System: the Experiences of Fifteen Fathers.' *International Journal of Disability, Development and Education 44,* 3, 229–241.

Bassin, D., Honey, M. and Mahrer Kaplan, M. (eds) (1994) *Representations of Motherhood.* New Haven: Yale University Press.

Benn, M. (1998) *Madonna and Child: Towards a New Politics on Motherhood.* London: Jonathan Cape.

Beresford, B., Sloper, P., Baldwin, S. and Newman, T. (1996) *What Works in Services for Families with a Disabled Child.* Barkingside: Barnardos.

Blum, N.J. and Mercugliano, M. (1997) 'Attention-Deficit/Hyperactivity Disorder.' In M.L. Batshaw (ed.) *Children with Disabilities,* 4th edn. London: Paul H. Books Publishing.

Boethius, G. and Rydlund, C. (1998) *Lycklig Varannan Onsdag. DAMP-mammor berättar.* Stockholm: Cura.

Booth, C.L. and Kelly, J.F. (1998) 'Child-Care Characteristics of Infants With and Without Special Needs: Comparisons and Concerns.' *Early Childhood Research Quarterly 13*, 4, 603–621.

Brown, C. (1998) *My Left Foot.* London: Vintage. (First published 1954.)

Buckley, S. (2000) 'Empowering Parents and Families – Is This the Way to Meet Family Needs?' *The Down Syndrome Educational Trust.* Accessed 19 February 2007 at http://information.downsed.org/library/periodicals/pdst-news/03/8/001/pdst-news-03-8-001-EN-GB.htm.

Cahill, B.M. and Glidden, L.M. (1996) 'Influence of Child Diagnosis on Family and Parental Functioning: Down Syndrome versus Other Disabilities.' *American Journal on Mental Retardation 101*, 2, 149–160.

Canning, K. (2004) 'Assessment without Service not Much Good.' *Irish Times,* 22 September, 14.

Carolan, M. (2000) 'Mother Power Wins over a Deaf State.' *Irish Times,* 7 October, 9.

Carolan, M. (2001) 'Judgment is Reserved on Sinnott Case Appeal.' *Irish Times,* 4 April, 4.

Carolan, M. (2004) 'Mother Wins Landmark Case for Her Son.' *Irish Times,* 11 March, 4.

Case, S. (2000) 'Refocusing on the Parent: What are the Social Issues of Concern for Parents of Disabled Children?' *Disability and Society 15*, 2, 271–292.

Central Statistics Office (2000) *That was Then, This is Now: Change in Ireland, 1949–1999.* Press statement, 24 February. Cork: CSO.

Central Statistics Office (2004a) *Women and Men in Ireland 2004.* Dublin: Stationery Office.

Central Statistics Office (2004b) *2002 Census of Population Volume 12 – Religion.* Press statement, 8 April 2004. Cork: CSO.

CHADD (2001) *Fact Sheet 5.* Accessed 19 February 2007 on www.help4adhd.org/en/treatment/coexisting/WWK5

Chodorow, N. (1978) *The Reproduction of Mothering. Psychoanalysis and the Sociology of Gender.* Berkeley, CA: University of California Press.

Conroy, P. (1999) 'From the Fifties to the Nineties: Social Policy Comes Out of the Shadows.' In G. Kiely, A. O'Donnell, P. Kennedy and S. Quin (eds) *Irish Social Policy in Context.* Dublin: University College Dublin.

Coulter, C. (2004) 'Legal Experts Say Disability Bill is Flawed.' *Irish Times,* 27 September, 7.

Croghan, R. and Miell, D. (1998) 'Strategies of Resistance: "'Bad" Mothers Dispute the Evidence.' *Feminism and Psychology 8*, 4, 445–465.

Dale, N. (1996) *Working with Families of Children with Special Needs – Partnership and Practice.* London: Routledge.

Dalley, G. (1996) *Ideologies of Caring. Rethinking Community and Collectivism,* 2nd edn. Basingstoke: MacMillan Press.

De Beauvoir, S. (1977) *The Second Sex*, transl. and ed. by H.M. Parshley. London: Vintage. (First published in French as *Le Deuxieme Sexe*, 1949.)

Deckmar, M. (2005) *My Son Fred – Living with Autism*, transl. by Ewa Wulkan. London: Jessica Kingsley Publishers. (First published in 1998 in Swedish as *Freds Bok: En mammas berättelse om när livet vänder*. Trångviken: Ord och Tanke.)

Department of Health (1983a) *The Education and Training of Severely and Profoundly Mentally Handicapped Children in Ireland. Report of a Working Party for the Minister of Education and the Minister for Health and Social Welfare*. Dublin: Stationery Office.

Department of Health (1983b) *Towards a Full Life. Green Paper on Services for Disabled People*. Dublin: Stationery Office.

Disability Act 2005. Dublin: Stationery Office.

Dowling, M. and Dolan, L. (2001) 'Families with Children with Disabilities – Inequalities and the Social Model.' *Disability and Society 16*, 1, 21–35.

Dumas, J.E., Wolf, L.C., Fisman, N.C. and Culligan, A. (1991) 'Parenting Stress, Child Behavior Problems, and Dysphoria in Parents of Children with Autism, Down Syndrome, Behavior Disorders, and Normal Development.' *Exceptionality 2*, 97–110.

Dwyer Brust, J., Leonard, B.J. and Sielaff, B.H. (1992) 'Maternal Time and the Care of Disabled Children.' *Public Health Nursing 9*, 3, 177–184.

Education for Persons with Special Educational Needs Act 2004. Dublin: Stationery Office.

Enright, A. (2004) *Making Babies: Stumbling into Motherhood*. London: Jonathan Cape.

EU Presidency (2004). 'Ireland's Economic Boom.' Accessed 19 February 2007 at www.eu2004.ie/templates/ standard.asp?sNavlocator=3, 242, 466.

Examiner (1997) 'State is Defeated by Brave Mother.' 7 February, 1.

Featherstone, B. (1997) '"I Wouldn't Do Your Job!" Women, Social Work and Child Abuse.' In W. Hollway and B. Featherstone (eds) *Mothering and Ambivalence*. London: Routledge.

Featherstone, B. (1999) 'Taking Mothering Seriously: The Implications for Child Protection.' *Child and Family Social Work 4*, 1, 43–53.

Firestone, S. (2003) *The Dialectic of Sex: The Case for Feminist Revolution*. New York: Farrar, Straus and Giroux.

Fitzgerald, M., Matthews, P., Birkbeck, G. and O'Connor, J. (2000) *Irish Families under Stress. Planning for the Future of Autistic Persons. A Prevalence and Psychological Study in the Eastern Health Board Area of Dublin* vol. 6. Dublin, Eastern Health Board.

Gottlieb, A.S. (1997) 'Single Mothers of Children with Developmental Disabilities: The Impact of Multiple Roles.' *Family Relations 46*, 1, 5–12.

Grant, G. and Ramcharan, P. (2001) 'Views and Experience of People with Intellectual Disabilities and their Families. (2) The Family Perspective.' *Journal of Applied Research in Intellectual Disabilities 14*, 364–380.

Gray, D.E. (1993) 'Perceptions of Stigma: The Parents of Autistic Children.' *Sociology of Health and Illness 15*, 1, 102–120.

Greenspan, M. (1998) 'Exceptional Mothering in a Normal World.' In C.G. Coll, J. Surrey and K. Weingarten (eds) *Mothering Against the Odds: Diverse Voices of Contemporary Mothers.* New York: Guildford Press.

Hanna, J. (1996) *The Friendship Tree. The Life and Poems of Davoren Hanna.* Dublin: New Island Books.

Haughey, N. (2003) 'Hypocrisy Behind the Hype.' *Irish Times*, 14 June, W1.

Hautamäki, A. (1997) 'Mothers – Stress, Stressors and Strain: Outcomes of a Cross-Nordic Study.' In B. Carpenter (ed.) *Families in Context: Emerging Trends in Family Support and Early Intervention.* London: David Fulton Publishers.

Hennessy, M. (2001) 'FF TDs Criticise Sinnott Case.' *Irish Times*, 23 March, 5.

Hewetson, A. (2002) *The Stolen Child: Aspects of Autism and Asperger Syndrome.* Westport: Greenwood Press.

Hewetson, A. (2005) *Laughter and Tears. A Family's Journey to Understanding Autism.* London: Jessica Kingsley Publishers.

Hoare, P., Harris, M., Jackson, P. and Kerley, S. (1998) 'A Community Survey of Children with Severe Intellectual Disability and Their Families: Psychological Adjustment, Carer Distress and the Effect of Respite Care.' *Journal of Intellectual Disability Research 42*, 3, 218–227.

Holland, K. (2004a) 'Mother Takes Health Board to Court over Help in Taking Care of Her Son.' *Irish Times*, 6 April, Health Supplement, 3.

Holland, K. (2004b) 'Mother Upset by Care Plans for Disabled Son.' *Irish Times*, 3 September, 5.

Home, A. (2002) 'Challenging Hidden Oppression: Mothers Caring for Children with Disabilities.' *Critical Social Work 2*, 2.

Horgan, G. (2004) 'Mothering in a Disabling Society.' In P. Kennedy (ed.) *Motherhood in Ireland.* Cork: Mercier Press.

Irish Constitution 1937. Dublin: Stationery Office.

Irish Examiner (2001) 'Mother Courage: Valerie Whelan Fights to Educate Her Autistic Son, Dara.' Feelgood Supplement, 2 November, 1.

Irish Times (2001a) 'Taking Action against a Sea of State Troubles.' 9 October, EL 5.

Healey, Y. (2001) 'A Sorry State of Affairs.' *Irish Times* 6 February pp.EL8–9.

Joesch, J.M and Smith, K.R. (1997) 'Children's Health and Their Mothers' Risk of Divorce or Separation.' *Social Biology 44*, 3–4, 159–169.

Kennedy, P. (2002) *Maternity in Ireland – a Woman-Centred Perspective.* Dublin: The Liffey Press.

Kennedy, P. (ed.) (2004) *Motherhood in Ireland.* Cork: Mercier Press.

Kiely, G. and Richardson, V. (1995) 'Family Policy in Ireland.' In I.C. McCarthy (ed.) *Irish Family Studies: Selected Papers.* Dublin: Family Studies Centre, UCD.

Kingsley, E.P. (1987) *Welcome to Holland.* Accessed 1 December 2006 at www.nas.com/ downsyn/ holland.html.

Kittay, E.F. (1999) '"Not My Way, Sesha, Your Way, Slowly": "Maternal Thinking" in the Raising of a Child with Profound Intellectual Disability.' In J.E. Hanigsberg and S. Ruddick (eds) *Mother Troubles. Rethinking Contemporary Maternal Dilemmas.* Boston: Beacon Press.

Kittay, E.F. (2002) 'When Caring Is Just and Justice is Caring: Justice and Mental Retardation.' In E.F. Kittay and E.K. Feder (eds) *The Subject of Care. Feminist Perspectives on Dependency.* New York: Rowman and Littlefield Publishers.

Knox, M., Parmenter, T., Atkinson, N. and Yazbeck, M. (2000) 'Family Control: The Views of Families Who have a Child with an Intellectual Disability.' *Journal of Applied Research in Intellectual Disabilities 13,* 17–28.

Ladd-Taylor, M. and Ulmansky, L. (1998) *'Bad' Mothers: The Politics of Blame in Twentieth-Century America.* New York: New York University Press.

Lagen om särskilt stöd och service till vissa funktionshindrade (1993) Stockholm: Regeringskansliet.

Landsman, G. (1998) 'Reconstructing Motherhood in the Age of "Perfect" Babies: Mother of Infants and Toddlers with Disabilities.' *Sign: Journal of Women in Culture and Society 24,* 1, 69–99.

Landsman, G. (1999) 'Does God Give Special Kids to Special Parents?' In L. Layne (ed.) *Transformative Motherhood: On Giving and Getting in a Consumer Culture.* New York: New York University Press.

Leach, P. and Jessel, C. (1997) *Baby and Child.* London: Penguin.

Leach, P. and Matthews, J. (2003) *Your Baby and Child.* London: Dorling Kindersley.

Lewis, S., Kagan, C. and Heaton, P. (2000) 'Managing Work-family Diversity for Parents of Disabled Children.' *Personnel Review 29,* 3, 417–430.

Lewis, S., Kagan, C., Heaton, P. and Cranshaw, M. (1999) 'Economic and Psychological Benefits from Employment: The Experiences and Perspectives of Mothers of Disabled Children.' *Disability and Society 14,* 4, 561–575.

Looney, F. (2005) *Misadventures in Motherhood: Life with The Small Girl, The Boy and The Toddler.* Dublin: O'Briens Press.

Lovenfosse, M. and Viney, L.L. (1999) 'Understanding and Helping Mothers of Children with "Special Needs" Using Personal Construct Group Work.' *Community Mental Health Journal 35,* 5, 431–442.

Lucey, A. (2003) 'Mother Says Funds Should be Spent on Our Disabled.' *Irish Times,* 17 June, 7.

Malacrida, C. (2003) *Cold Comfort: Mothers, Professionals, and Attention Deficit Disorder.* Toronto: University of Toronto Press.

McCarthy, I.C. (ed.) (1995) *Irish Family Studies: Selected Papers.* Dublin: Family Studies Centre, University College Dublin.

McCormack, B. (1987) 'The Delivery Agency: A Service Model from Ireland.' Seminar, *The Status of the European Citizen with a Mental Handicap,* 10–12 June, Llandudno, Wales.

McDonnell, J.T. (1991) 'Mothering an Autistic Child: Reclaiming the Voice of the Mother.' In B. O'Daly and M.T. Reddy (eds) *Narrating Mothers. Theorizing Maternal Subjectivities.* Knoxville: University of Tennessee Press.

McDonnell, J.T. (1993) *News From the Border.* New York: Ticknor and Fields.

McGlinchey, A. (2001) 'Adaptation of Parents with Children with Autistic Spectrum Disorders.' Unpublished PhD thesis in Psychology, University College Dublin.

McLaughlin, J. (2003) 'Screening Networks: Shared Agendas in Feminist and Disability Movement Challenges to Antenatal Screening and Abortion.' Unpublished paper presented at *Gender and Power in the New Europe, the 5th European Feminist Research Conference,* August 20–24, Lund University, Sweden.

Miller, F.A. and Rock, M. (1998) 'Mothering the Well-Born.' In S. Abbey and A. O'Reilly (eds) *Redefining Motherhood: Changing Identities and Patterns.* Toronto: Second Story Press.

Miller, T. (2005) *Making Sense of Motherhood: A Narrative Approach.* Cambridge: Cambridge University Press.

Murray, P. (2000) 'Disabled Children, Parents and Professionals: Partnership on Whose Terms?' *Disability and Society 15,* 4, 683–698.

Musgrave, D. (2001) 'The Mother of All Battles when State Ignores my Son's Plight.' *Irish Examiner,* 2 August, 16.

NAMHI News (2002) Submission to the Department of Justice, Equality and Law Reform on the Disability Bill 2001, February. Dublin: National Association for Intellectual Learning Disabilities in Ireland (NAMHI). Accessed 19 February 2007 at www.inclusionireland

Naughton, P. (1993) 'State Deprived Handicapped Cork Boy of His Rights.' *Cork Examiner,* 28 May, 6.

Nolan, L. (2004) *Once in August Long Ago. A Week in the Life of an Autistic Boy.* Loughrea, Ireland: Greylake Publications.

Nordin-Olson, E. (2004) 'Ledare.' *Ögonblick* (1), January, 3.

O'Brien, C. (2004) 'Only 25% of Services for Disabled up to Standard, Survey Finds.' *Irish Times,* 25 February, 3.

O'Brien, C. (2005a) '€19 a week for parents of under-sixes.' *Irish Times,* Budget Supplement, 8 December, 3.

O'Brien, C. (2005b) 'Family "devastated" at move to take children into care.' *Irish Times,* 5 March, 1.

O'Brien, C. (2005c) 'Judge says 5 children can be returned to their parents.' *Irish Times*, 11 March, 1.

O'Donoghue, Marie (undated) Background to the consitutional challenge for educational entitlements – Paul O'Donoghue (a minor) V. the Minister for Education, The minister for Health, Ireland and The Attorney General. Reference: High Court 75.JR/1992 Supreme Court 6 Feb. 1997. Handout distributed through Embrace (former Association for the Severely and Profoundly Mentally Handicapped), Cork.

Olsson, M.B. (2004) *Parents of Children with Intellectual Disabilities.* Göteborg: Department of Psychology, Göteborg University.

Olsson, M.B. and Hwang, C.P. (2003) 'Influence of Macrostructure of Society on the Life Situation of Families with a Child with Intellectual Disability: Sweden as an Example.' *Journal of Intellectual Disability Research 47*, 4/5, 328–341.

O'Reilly, A. (2006) *Rocking the Cradle: Thoughts on Motherhood, Feminism and the Possibility of Empowered Mothering.* Toronto: Demeter Press.

Persson, E. (2004) 'Mycket ork för att orka.' *Östgöta-Correspondenten*, 5 March, A10.

Pillinger, J. (2002) 'Disability and the Quality of Services: Irish and European Perspectives.' Policy Institute Working Paper presented on behalf of the National Disability Authority, 16 April. Dublin: Trinity College, Dublin.

Prime Time Investigates (2004) RTE, 10 May.

Rapp, R. (1995). 'Risky Business: Genetic Counselling in a Shifting World.' In J. Schneider and R. Rapp (eds) *Articulating Hidden Histories: Exploring the Influence of Eric R. Wolf.* Berkeley, CA: University of California Press.

Read, J. (1991) 'There was Never Really any Choice – The Experience of Mothers of Disabled Children in the UK.' *Women's Studies International Forum 14*, 6, 561–571.

Read, J. (2000) *Disability, the Family and Society: Listening to Mothers.* Buckingham: Open University Press.

Read, J. and Clements, L. (2001) *Disabled Children and the Law: Research and Good Practice.* London: Jessica Kingsley Publishers.

Redmond, B. (1993) 'Listening to Parents: The Aspirations, Expectations and Anxieties of Parents about their Teenager with Learning Disability.' Unpublished thesis, Family Studies Centre, University College, Dublin.

Redmond, B. and Richardson, V. (2003) 'Just Getting on with It: Exploring the Service Needs of Mothers Who Care for Young Children with Severe/Profound and Life-threatening Intellectual Disability.' *Journal of Applied Research in Intellectual Disabilities 16*, 3: 205–218.

Ribbens, J. (1994) *Mothers and their Children. A Feminist Sociology of Childrearing.* London: Sage.

Rich, A. (1977) *Of Woman Born: Motherhood as Experience and Institution.* London: Virago.

Ring, E. (2003) 'Over 50% parents smack their children, survey finds.' *The Irish Examiner*. Accessed 4 July 2003 at http://archives.tcm.ie/irishexaminer/2003/07/04/story420964762.asp

Roche, B. (2004) 'Sinnott Banishes Election Defeat Memory.' *Irish Times*. Accessed 15 June 2004 at www.ireland.com/newspaper/ireland/2004/0615/pf776055193EL5SOUTH.html.

Roizen, N.J. (1997) 'Down Syndrome.' In M.L. Batshaw (ed.) *Children with Disabilities*. London: Paul H. Books Publishing.

Ruddick, S. (1989) *Maternal Thinking: Toward a Politics of Peace*. New York: Ballantine Books.

Ryan, A. (1999) *Walls of Silence*. Callan, Kilkenny: Red Lion Press.

Ryan, S. (2005) '"Busy Behaviour" in the "Land of the Golden M": Going Out with Learning Disabled Children in Public Places.' *Journal of Applied Research in Intellectual Disabilities 18*, 65–74.

Ryde-Brandt, B. (1991) 'Defence Strategies and Anxiety in Mothers of Disabled Children.' *European Journal of Personality 5*, 5, 367–377.

Sanders, J.L. and Morgan, S.B. (1997). 'Family Stress and Adjustment as Perceived by Parents of Children with Autism or Down Syndrome: Implications for Intervention.' *Child and Family Behavior Therapy 19*, 4, 15–32.

Shanahan, C. (2002) 'Treatment of Disabled People Slammed by UN.' *Irish Examiner*, 22 May, 1.

Sharpley, C.F., Bitsika,V. and Efremidis, B. (1997) 'Influence of Gender, Parental Health, and Perceived Expertise of Assistance upon Stress, Anxiety, and Depression among Parents of Children with Autism.' *Journal of Intellectual and Developmental Disability 22*, 1, 19–28.

Sheahan, F. (2003) 'Courts Only Way to Get Rights for Our Special-needs Children.' *Irish Examiner*, 26 June, 1.

Shearn, J. and Todd, S. (2000) 'Maternal Employment and Family Responsibilities: The Perspectives of Mothers of Children with Intellectual Disabilities.' *Journal of Applied Research in Intellectual Disabilities 13*, 109–131.

Sloper, P. (1999) 'Models of Service Support for Parents of Disabled Children. What do We Know? What do We Need to Know?' *Child: Care, Health and Development 25*, 2, 85–99.

Snell, S.A. and Rosen, K.H. (1997) 'Parents of Special Needs Children Mastering the Job of Parenting.' *Contemporary Family Therapy 19*, 3, 425–442.

Stalker, K. and Robinson, C. (1994) 'Parents' View of Different Respite Care Services.' *Mental Handicap Research 7*, 2, 97–117.

Statistics Sweden (2006) *Pressmeddelande från SCB*. 14 September, Nr 2006, 228.

Tarrant, S.K. (2002) 'The Maternal Metamorphosis: Experiences of Fourteen Women Parenting Children with High Functioning Autism in North Central Victoria.'

Unpublished thesis, Department of Public Health, La Trobe University, Bendigo, Australia.

Todd, S. and Jones, S. (2003) '"Mum's the Word!" Maternal Accounts of Dealings with the Professional World.' *Journal of Applied Research in Intellectual Disabilities 16*, 3, 229–244.

Toolan, D. (2003) 'Hypocrisy on Rights of Disabled People Needs to be Exposed.' *Irish Times*, 12 June, 14.

Traustadottir, R. (1991) 'Mothers Who Care. Gender, Disability, and Family Life.' *Journal of Family Issues 12*, 2, 211–228.

Trute, B. (1995) 'Gender Differences in the Psychological Adjustment of Parents of Young, Developmentally Disabled Children.' *Journal of Child Psychology and Psychiatry 36*, 7, 1225–1242.

Veisson, M. (1999) 'Depression Symptoms and Emotional States in Parents of Disabled and Non-disabled Children.' *Social, Behavior and Personality 27*, 1, 87–98.

Waltzer, S. (1996) 'Thinking About the Baby: Gender and Divisions of Infant Care.' *Social Problems 43*, 2.

Warfield Erickson, M. and Hauser-Cram, P. (1996) 'Child Care Needs, Arrangements, and Satisfaction of Mothers of Children with Developmental Disabilities.' *Mental Retardation 34*, 5, 294–302.

Warfield Erickson, M., Hauser-Cram, P., Wyngaarden Krauss, M., Upshur, C.C. and Shonkoff, J.P. (1999) 'Adaptation during Early Childhood among Mothers of Children with Disabilities.' *Developmental and Behavioral Pediatrics 20*, 1, 9–16.

Widdows, J. (1997) *A Special Need for Inclusion: Children with Disabilities, their Families and Everyday Life.* London: The Children's Society.

Subject Index

Author Index

21646252R00120

Printed in Great Britain
by Amazon